Thembalethu John Kumatana

Footsteps of Hopelessness

Copyright

Copyright 2025
Thembalethu John Kumatana
The right of Thembalethu John Kumatana to be identified as the author of this work through the
Copyright, Designs and Patents Act 1988.
All Rights Reserved
No reproduction, copy or transmission of this publication may be made without written permission.
No paragraph of this publication may be reproduced, copied or transmitted save with the written permission of the author or by the provisions
of the Copyright Act 1956 (as amended).
Any person who commits any unauthorised act about this publication may be liable to criminal prosecution and civil claims for damages.
First Published in 2025

Proofreading and Editing by Busy Bee Editing
(www.busybeeediting.co.za)

Walk Towards Healing

Remember, hope is not the absence of shadows but the light that guides you through them. You are not alone, and you are stronger than you think. Take a breath and let the journey of healing begin.

I would love to hear from you. Please share your thoughts and feedback on my book by email, Facebook, Instagram or LinkedIn.

footstepsbookseries@gmail.com

Facebook page: footsteps Book Series

Instagram: footstepsbooks

LinkedIn: Footsteps Book Series

Contents

Copyright 1
Walk Towards Healing 2
Preface 6
Why Hopelessness? 11
What is Hopelessness? 12
My Experience of Hopelessness 13
What Are the Root Causes of Hopelessness? 16
Losing a Loved One 17
Losing Parents 19
Absent Parents 21
Relationship Changes 24
Impact of Rejection 25
Traumatic Experiences and Hopelessness 28
The Deep Impact of Trauma 28
Emotional Overwhelm and Negative Beliefs 30
Isolation and Identity Loss 33
Finding the Path to Healing 36
Holding on to Hope 39
The Alcohol Mindset 41
Drug Abuse 45
Lack of Education 46
Lack of Trust 47
Lack of Belief 49
Lack of Confidence 50
Lack of Motivation 52
Chronic Stress 53

Mental Health Disorders	55
Lack of Support	57
Forms of Hopelessness	58
Detachment	58
Forsakenness	61
Lack of Inspiration	63
Powerlessness	65
Oppression	67
Limitedness	70
Captivity	72
Doom	74
Discrimination	75
Experience	78
The Poverty of the Pocket	82
The Poverty of the Mind	84
Six Signs of Poverty of the Mind - Not Limited	85
Feeling Unworthy	85
A Fear of Success and Abundance	87
Passivity	89
A Debt Mentality	90
A Small Vision	92
Fear of Failure	94
A Victim Mentality	95
Being Taken Advantage of	97
Bad Leadership	99
Exploitation	101
How to Deal With Hopelessness	102
Steps to Take When Dealing With Hopelessness	105

Acknowledge the Feelings and Accept 105
Hopelessness is Temporary................................ 106
Name Your Feelings 107
Practise Gratitude 109
Control.. 111
How Far Have You Come?.................................. 113
Healthy Eating 114
Make Space to Grieve 115
Patience... 117
Do Not Overthink It 118
Staying Present 120
Prioritise Meaningful Relationships................... 121
Reach out for Support....................................... 123
Practise Self-Care 125
Talk to a Mental Health Professional................. 127
Motivation on How to Deal With Hopelessness 129
Salute! 132
Jeremiah 29:11... 133

Preface

Sitting down to write this book, I reflected on the journey that led me here. The **Footsteps of Hopelessness** that I witnessed and experienced in my own life and the lives of those around me have left a lasting impact on me. Through these experiences, I have understood hopelessness's profound and often devastating effects on individuals and communities.

In writing this book, I aim to illuminate the struggles and challenges those trapped in a cycle of hopelessness face. I want to explore the roots of this despair and examine how it manifests in our lives. Through the stories and experiences shared within these pages, I hope to glimpse and reflect on the lives of those who feel there is no way out.

The idea for this book came to me during a particularly dark period when I felt overwhelmed by a sense of hopelessness. I found myself questioning my purpose and my place in the world, and I felt as though I was stuck in a never-ending cycle of despair.

During this time, I realised the power of sharing our stories and experiences with others and the healing that can come from connecting with those who have walked a similar path.

In writing about the **Footsteps of Hopelessness**, I hope to offer a sense of comfort and solace to those who may be struggling with similar feelings. I want to create a space for open and honest dialogue about our struggles and ways to find hope and healing during our darkest moments. I encourage you to reflect on your experiences with hopelessness and consider how you can find hope and healing during despair.

In 2022, after acquiring my diploma in counselling, I found myself contemplating how I could positively impact the community by providing counselling support to those who cannot afford the hefty charges associated with therapy services. It became evident that mental health support should be accessible to everyone, regardless of their financial situation. This realisation sparked my passion for creating a simple counselling guide for those in need. The importance of mental health cannot be overstated, yet many individuals are unable to seek professional help due to financial constraints. This disparity in access to mental health services underscores the need for alternative solutions that can bridge the gap and provide support to those who are struggling with their mental well-being.

Creating a simple counselling guide involves distilling the key principles and techniques of counselling into an accessible format that individuals seeking support can easily understand and apply. The guide empowers individuals to navigate their emotions, thoughts, and challenges constructively and healthily, even without professional counselling services.

One of the fundamental aspects of the simple counselling guide is promoting self-awareness and self-reflection. By encouraging individuals to explore their thoughts and feelings, the guide will help them gain insights into their inner world and identify the patterns contributing to their distress. Self-awareness is a crucial first step towards personal growth and emotional well-being. Additionally, the guide emphasises the importance of developing coping strategies and self-care practices that can help individuals manage stress, anxiety, and other mental health issues. The guide aims to create a supportive network to complement the self-help strategies outlined by connecting individuals to available resources.

Overall, the goal of the simple counselling guide is to empower individuals to take charge of their mental health and well-being, even in the absence of professional counselling services. By providing accessible and practical guidance, the guide seeks to make a positive impact on the lives of those who are struggling with mental health issues and cannot afford traditional therapy services.

The creation of a simple counselling guide for those in need represents a proactive and compassionate approach to addressing the mental health challenges faced by many individuals in our community. The guide aims to empower individuals to navigate their mental health journey with resilience and strength by promoting self-awareness, coping strategies, communication skills, and access to resources. Together, we can work towards a future where mental health support is accessible to all, regardless of financial barriers.

Growing up in the Xhosa culture, I was exposed to a worldview where counselling was perceived as a service reserved for the affluent and not commonly embraced within African communities. In my cultural upbringing, the primary form of mental health support was through social workers, with counselling being an unfamiliar concept. This cultural perspective shaped my understanding of mental health and help-seeking behaviours, highlighting the need to explore and challenge traditional perceptions to foster a more inclusive approach to well-being within the Xhosa culture.

In Xhosa culture, community and familial support are central to addressing personal challenges and emotional struggles. Social workers are often seen as key figures who provide practical assistance and guidance to individuals and families facing social issues, such as poverty, domestic violence, or child welfare concerns. While social workers offer valuable support in addressing external challenges, focusing on emotional well-being and mental health may not always receive the same attention. The perception of counselling as a service for wealthy or privileged individuals reflects broader societal attitudes towards mental health within African communities.

Stigma, misconceptions, and limited awareness about mental health issues can contribute to people's reluctance to seek professional counselling support. Additionally, the historical lack of representation of counselling services within traditional African healing practices may further contribute to the underutilisation of counselling resources.

As I embarked on my journey in the field of counselling, I gained a deeper understanding of mental health practices; I began to question and challenge the cultural norms that had shaped my initial perceptions. I recognised the importance of integrating culturally relevant approaches to mental health support within the Xhosa community, acknowledging the rich traditions and healing practices that can complement modern counselling techniques. In redefining the role of counselling within the Xhosa culture, it is essential to emphasise the value of mental health and emotional well-being as integral components of overall wellness. By promoting awareness, education, and destigmatisation of mental health issues, we can empower individuals within the Xhosa community to prioritise their psychological well-being and seek appropriate support when needed.

Moreover, incorporating counselling services that are culturally sensitive and responsive to the unique needs and beliefs of the Xhosa culture can help bridge the gap between traditional healing practices and modern mental health interventions. By fostering collaborations between counsellors, traditional healers, community leaders, and social workers, we can create a holistic support system that addresses the diverse needs of individuals within the Xhosa community. The evolution of mental health support within the Xhosa culture requires a shift in perceptions, attitudes, and practices surrounding counselling and help-seeking behaviours.

By challenging traditional views, promoting cultural inclusivity, and advocating for accessible and culturally relevant mental health services, we can create a more supportive and empowering environment for individuals to prioritise their mental well-being. Together, we can honour the rich heritage of the Xhosa culture while embracing the importance of mental health and emotional wellness for all.

I invite you to join me on this journey as we explore the *Footsteps of Hopelessness* together and discover the light that can shine through even the darkest times. May this book serve as a beacon of hope for all who feel lost in the darkness and remind us that even in our darkest moments, there is always a glimmer of light to guide us forward.

Why Hopelessness?

Writing a counselling guide on hopelessness is driven by deep empathy and a desire to support those struggling with despair. For me, the motivation comes from a genuine wish to offer guidance, comfort, and practical strategies to individuals facing challenges related to hopelessness. By sharing insights, coping mechanisms, and therapeutic approaches, I aim to provide a lifeline for those in need and instil hope in their hearts. Contributing to a community's well-being is a noble pursuit that can have a ripple effect of positive change.

By writing a counselling guide on hopelessness, I am offering a valuable resource to individuals grappling with difficult emotions and circumstances. Giving back is a way to support and uplift the community, fostering a sense of connection and solidarity among those facing similar struggles. As parents, one of the greatest legacies we can leave for our children is the gift of knowledge and compassion.

By writing a counselling guide on hopelessness, I am creating a lasting resource that our children can turn to for guidance and support long after we are gone. This book serves as a token of wisdom and empathy and is a testament to our values and beliefs, ensuring that our influence continues to shape and inspire future generations. I aim to empower individuals to navigate challenges and find hope during despair, a powerful way to impact society positively. Through writing, I am equipping readers with tools, strategies, and insights to help them overcome feelings of hopelessness and build resilience.

By empowering others to seek help, practise self-care, and cultivate a sense of optimism, I am building a community of strength and support that can endure through generations.

Writing a counselling guide on hopelessness is a meaningful way to give back to the community and leave a valuable legacy for future generations, including one's children.

By offering support, guidance, and hope to those in need, I am trying to make a profound impact on the lives of others while ensuring that their wisdom and compassion will continue to inspire and uplift individuals long after they are gone. Through writing, I am sowing the seeds of hope and resilience that will flourish and endure for years.

What is Hopelessness?

Helplessness is feeling powerless or unable to control a situation or circumstance. It is a common human experience that can manifest in various aspects of life, such as relationships, work, health, and personal challenges. Understanding the concept of helplessness and its impact on individuals is crucial to addressing and overcoming it effectively. One of the key factors contributing to helplessness is the perception of a lack of control. When individuals believe they cannot influence their circumstances or outcomes, they may experience a sense of helplessness. This feeling can be exacerbated by external factors such as societal norms, economic constraints, or oppressive systems that limit individuals' agency and autonomy.

Additionally, past experiences of failure or trauma can also contribute to a sense of helplessness, as individuals may develop a learnt helplessness mindset that perpetuates feelings of powerlessness. Helplessness can have significant adverse effects on individuals' mental and emotional well-being. It can lead to feelings of anxiety, depression, and low self-esteem as individuals struggle to cope with challenges and setbacks. Helplessness can also impact individuals' motivation and ability to act, as they may feel overwhelmed by a sense of futility and resignation.

In extreme cases, prolonged feelings of helplessness can contribute to the development of mental health disorders and contribute to a cycle of negative thinking and behaviour. Overcoming helplessness requires a combination of self-awareness, resilience, and support. Individuals can begin by identifying the sources of their helplessness and challenging negative beliefs and thought patterns that contribute to feelings of powerlessness.

Developing a sense of self-efficacy and agency is crucial in building resilience and coping mechanisms to navigate challenging situations. Seeking support from friends, family, or mental health professionals can also provide individuals with the tools and resources needed to address feelings of helplessness and regain a sense of control over their lives.

Helplessness is a complex and multifaceted experience that profoundly affects individuals' well-being. By understanding the underlying causes of helplessness and implementing strategies to address and overcome it, individuals can cultivate a sense of empowerment and agency in their lives. Through self-awareness, resilience, and support, individuals can break free from the cycle of helplessness and create a more positive and fulfilling life.

My Experience of Hopelessness

As someone who has seen the destructive power of hopelessness firsthand, we must reach out to struggling people and offer our support and compassion. A simple act of kindness, a listening ear, or a reassuring presence can make a world of difference to someone feeling lost and alone. By extending a hand of friendship and understanding, we can help break the cycle of hopelessness and offer hope to those who need it most.

Hopelessness is a powerful emotion that can consume individuals when they feel isolated, abandoned, and overwhelmed by life's challenges. I have witnessed firsthand the devastating effects of hopelessness on someone who feels like they have no one to turn to, no shoulder to cry on, and no support system to rely on. In those moments, the world seems lonely and unforgiving, where hopelessness thrives and takes hold of one's spirit.

When a person is engulfed in hopelessness, it can feel as though the weight of the world is bearing on their shoulders, suffocating them with despair and helplessness. Every obstacle, setback, and disappointment can seem insurmountable, leaving them feeling defeated and drained of any motivation or will to keep going.

The sense of isolation and loneliness can further exacerbate these feelings, creating a vicious cycle of despair that is difficult to break free from. Without a support system or someone to confide in, the burden of hopelessness can become unbearable. The lack of a listening ear or a comforting presence can intensify feelings of loneliness and detachment, making it even harder to see a way out of the darkness. In these moments, it can be easy to believe that the whole world is against you, that there is no light at the end of the tunnel, and that hope is nothing but a distant memory. Every step you take is heavy with despair and uncertainty, dragging you further into a dark and lonely place.

I know that feeling all too well. It is like being stuck in quicksand, sinking deeper and deeper with each passing moment. You try to claw your way out, but the more you struggle, the more you realise that there is no escape. The weight of your worries and fears pulls you down, suffocating you in a sea of doubt and despair.

I remember feeling lost in a maze of hopelessness, unable to find my way out. Every path I took seemed to lead me further into the darkness, away from the light of hope and happiness. I felt trapped in a never-ending cycle of negativity, unable to break free from its suffocating grip. But then, something changed. I realised I did not have to stay stuck in that place of hopelessness. I could take a different path, stepping out of the shadows and into the light. It was not easy, and it took time and effort, but slowly, I began to see a glimmer of hope on the horizon.

I started surrounding myself with positive influences, people who lifted me and encouraged me to keep moving forward. I began to focus on the things that brought me joy and fulfilment rather than dwelling on the things that brought me down. I learnt to let go of the past and embrace the present, live in the moment, and appreciate life's beauty. Slowly but surely, I began to see a change.

The **Footsteps of Hopelessness** that had once weighed me down began to fade, replaced by the lightness of hope and possibility. I started to believe in myself again and see the potential for a brighter future.

So, if you ever find yourself walking in the **Footsteps of Hopelessness**, remember that you can change your path. You do not have to stay stuck in that dark and lonely place. You can step out of the shadows and into the light to embrace hope and possibility again. It will not be easy and will not happen overnight, but with determination and perseverance, you can break free from the chains of hopelessness and find your way back to a place of light and joy. So, take that first step and keep moving forward. The journey may be extended and challenging, but the destination is worth it.

What Are the Root Causes of Hopelessness?

Hopelessness is a complex and pervasive emotion that can have a profound impact on an individual's mental health and well-being. It is a feeling of despair, helplessness, and lack of optimism about the future. While various factors can trigger hopelessness, several root causes are commonly associated with this emotion. One of the primary root causes of hopelessness is a sense of powerlessness. When individuals feel that they have no control over their circumstances or that their efforts will not lead to positive outcomes, they may experience feelings of hopelessness.

This can be particularly true when external factors, such as systemic inequalities or oppressive social structures, limit individuals' ability to effect change in their lives.

Another common root cause of hopelessness is a lack of support and connection with others. Human beings are social creatures, and our relationships with others are crucial to our emotional well-being. When individuals feel isolated, disconnected, or unsupported by those around them, they may struggle to maintain a sense of hope for the future. This can especially be true in times of crisis or hardship when the absence of a strong support network can exacerbate feelings of hopelessness.

Additionally, traumatic experiences and adverse life events can also serve as root causes of hopelessness. Individuals who have experienced significant trauma, such as abuse, loss, or violence, may struggle to maintain a sense of hope in the face of ongoing challenges. Trauma can profoundly impact a person's sense of self-worth, safety, and trust in others, leading to feelings of hopelessness and despair. Furthermore, chronic stress and ongoing struggles can contribute to feelings of hopelessness when individuals face persistent challenges, such as financial difficulties, health problems, or relationship issues. They may feel overwhelmed and hopeless about overcoming these obstacles.

The cumulative impact of ongoing stressors can erode a person's sense of optimism and resilience, making it difficult to maintain hope for the future. Factors such as powerlessness, lack of support, trauma, and chronic stress can all contribute to feelings of despair and helplessness. Recognising and addressing these root causes is essential in helping individuals navigate their emotions and cultivate a sense of hope for the future. By addressing the underlying factors contributing to hopelessness, individuals can begin healing and rebuilding their sense of optimism and resilience.

Losing a Loved One

The death of a loved one is a profound and harrowing experience that can have a lasting impact on an individual's emotional well-being. The loss of someone close can trigger a range of complex emotions, including grief, sadness, and a profound sense of emptiness. In many cases, the death of a loved one can also lead to feelings of hopelessness as individuals struggle to come to terms with their loss and find a way forward.

The death of a loved one often triggers intense feelings of grief and sadness. The profound sense of loss and emptiness that accompanies bereavement can be overwhelming, leaving individuals struggling to cope with their emotions. This overwhelming grief can contribute to feelings of hopelessness as individuals grapple with the reality of their loved one's absence and the impact it has on their lives.

The death of a loved one can create a profound sense of emptiness and loneliness in individuals' lives. The absence of the person who has passed away can leave a void that feels impossible to fill, leading to feelings of isolation and disconnection. This sense of emptiness and loneliness can exacerbate feelings of hopelessness as individuals struggle to find meaning and purpose in their lives without their loved ones by their side.

Losing a loved one can also result in a loss of support and connection. The person who has passed away may have been a source of comfort, understanding, and companionship for a person, and their absence can leave a significant void in the individual's life. This loss of support and connection can contribute to feelings of hopelessness, as individuals feel adrift and alone in their grief. The death of a loved one can also prompt individuals to question their beliefs and search for meaning in the face of loss. The profound impact of death can lead individuals to grapple with existential questions about life, death, and the nature of existence.

This search for meaning during grief can be a challenging and disorienting process, contributing to feelings of hopelessness and despair. While the death of a loved one can cause feelings of hopelessness, it is essential to recognise that grief is a natural and necessary process of healing. By allowing oneself to grieve and seeking support from others, individuals can begin to navigate their feelings of loss and find a way forward. Connecting with others who have experienced similar losses, engaging in self-care practices, and seeking professional help when needed can all be valuable strategies for coping with grief and finding hope during loss.

The death of a loved one can cause profound feelings of hopelessness as individuals grapple with overwhelming grief, a sense of emptiness and loneliness, loss of support and connection, questioning of beliefs and meaning, and the challenges of navigating grief. It is essential to acknowledge the impact of loss on individuals' emotional well-being and to provide support and resources to help them cope with their grief and find hope in the aftermath of loss. By honouring the memory of their loved one, seeking support from others, and engaging in self-care practices, individuals can begin to heal and find a sense of hope and resilience in the face of loss.

Losing Parents

The loss of parents is a deeply profound and emotionally challenging experience that can have a lasting impact on individuals. Parents play a significant role in shaping our lives by providing love, guidance, and support throughout our formative years. When individuals lose their parents, they often face a range of complex emotions, including grief, sadness, and a profound sense of loss. Losing parents can result in a profound sense of loss that can be difficult to comprehend or process fully.

Parents are often seen as pillars of strength and sources of unconditional love and support, and their absence can leave individuals feeling adrift and vulnerable.

The loss of this foundational relationship can lead to feelings of hopelessness as individuals struggle to come to terms with the void left by their parents' passing. Losing parents can also prompt significant changes in individuals' identities and roles within their family and broader community.

Parents often play a central role in shaping their children's sense of self and providing a sense of continuity and connection to one's past and heritage. When parents pass away, individuals may grapple with questions of identity and belonging, leading to feelings of disorientation and hopelessness. The death of parents can trigger intense emotional turmoil and grief as individuals navigate the complex emotions associated with loss.

Grief is a multifaceted process that can involve feelings of sadness, anger, guilt, and confusion. The overwhelming nature of grief can contribute to feelings of hopelessness as individuals struggle to make sense of their emotions and find a way forward in the absence of their parents.

Losing parents can also significantly change individuals' support systems and social networks. Parents often serve as primary sources of emotional and practical support, and their absence can leave individuals feeling isolated and vulnerable. The loss of this crucial support system can exacerbate feelings of hopelessness as individuals grapple with the challenges of navigating their grief without the presence of their parents. While losing parents can cause feelings of hopelessness, individuals need to recognise that grief is a natural and necessary process of healing.

By allowing themselves to grieve, seeking support from others, and engaging in self-care practices, individuals can begin to navigate their feelings of loss and find a way forward.

Connecting with others who have experienced similar losses, honouring the memory of their parents, and seeking professional help when needed can all be valuable strategies for coping with grief and finding hope during such a significant loss.

Losing parents can be a profoundly challenging and emotionally overwhelming experience that can cause feelings of hopelessness as individuals grapple with profound loss, changes in identity and roles, emotional turmoil and grief, support system changes, and the search for meaning and hope. It is essential to acknowledge the impact of losing parents on individuals' emotional well-being and to provide support and resources to help them cope with their grief and find hope in the aftermath of such a significant loss. By honouring the memory of their parents, seeking support from others, and engaging in self-care practices, individuals can begin to heal and find a sense of hope and resilience in the face of losing their parents.

Absent Parents

Having parents who are not involved in one's life can be a harrowing and emotionally challenging experience that can have a lasting impact on individuals. Parental absence can take many forms, including physical absence, emotional neglect, or lack of support and guidance. When individuals grow up without the presence and involvement of their parents, they may experience a range of complex emotions, including sadness, anger, and a profound sense of emptiness. Growing up without the involvement of parents can create a profound emotional void and sense of loneliness in individuals' lives.

Parents are often seen as primary sources of love, support, and guidance, and their absence can leave individuals feeling adrift and disconnected. The lack of emotional connection and parental nurturing can contribute to feelings of hopelessness as individuals struggle to fill the void left by their absence. Absent parents can significantly impact individuals' sense of self-worth and identity.

Parents play a crucial role in shaping their children's self-esteem, beliefs, and values, and their absence can leave individuals questioning their worth and value. The lack of parental involvement can lead to feelings of inadequacy and self-doubt, contributing to a sense of hopelessness as individuals struggle to find a sense of purpose and belonging without parental support. Growing up without involved parents can also result in trust and attachment issues in individuals. The lack of consistent and nurturing relationships with parents can make it difficult for individuals to trust others and form secure attachments.

This can lead to difficulties in creating and maintaining healthy relationships, exacerbating feelings of loneliness and isolation and contributing to a sense of hopelessness as individuals struggle to connect with others. The absence of parents can trigger intense emotional turmoil and grief as individuals grapple with the complex emotions associated with parental absence.

Feelings of sadness, anger, and confusion may arise as individuals process the impact of growing up without the presence of their parents. The overwhelming nature of this emotional turmoil can contribute to feelings of hopelessness as individuals struggle to make sense of their experiences and find a way forward. While having absent parents can cause feelings of hopelessness, individuals need to recognise that healing is possible.

By seeking support from others, engaging in therapy or counselling, and practising self-care and self-compassion, individuals can begin to navigate the emotional impact of parental absence and find hope amid their struggles. Connecting with supportive friends, mentors, or community resources and exploring one's strengths and resilience can also be valuable strategies for coping with the challenges of growing up without involved parents, thereby finding hope and healing.

Having parents who are not involved in one's life can be a profoundly challenging and emotionally overwhelming experience that can cause feelings of hopelessness as individuals grapple with emotional voids and loneliness. That may negatively impact their self-worth and identity, cause trust and attachment issues, emotional turmoil and grief, and hamper the search for healing and hope.

It is essential to acknowledge the impact of parental absence on individuals' emotional well-being and to provide support and resources to help them cope with the emotional challenges of growing up without involved parents. By seeking support, practising self-care, and exploring opportunities for healing and growth, individuals can begin to navigate the impact of parental absence and find hope and resilience in the face of their struggles.

Relationship Changes

Experiencing changes in a relationship can be a significant source of hopelessness and emotional distress. Whether it is the end of a romantic partnership, the breakdown of a friendship, or strained family dynamics, relationship changes can leave individuals feeling lost, confused, and overwhelmed. Acknowledging and addressing these feelings of hopelessness is essential to navigate the challenges and emerge stronger on the other side.

When faced with relationship changes that trigger feelings of hopelessness, it is necessary to allow yourself to process and express your emotions. When relationships change, it is normal to feel a range of emotions, such as sadness, anger, guilt, or loneliness. Permit yourself to grieve the loss, whether it is the end of a relationship or a shift in dynamics, and seek support from trusted friends, family members, or a therapist to help you navigate through this difficult time. It is also important to practise self-care and self-compassion during relationship changes.

Be gentle with yourself and avoid self-blame or negative self-talk. Engage in activities that bring comfort and joy, such as exercise, hobbies, or spending time with loved ones. Taking care of your physical and emotional well-being can help you build resilience and cope with feelings of hopelessness that may arise from relationship changes. Furthermore, communication can be key in navigating through relationship changes. Try to have open and honest conversations with the other party involved to express your feelings, concerns, and needs. Effective communication can clarify misunderstandings, address underlying issues, and pave the way for healing and reconciliation. However, setting boundaries and prioritising your well-being in interactions with others is essential. Seeking professional help, such as therapy or counselling, can also be beneficial in processing and coping with feelings of hopelessness related to relationship changes.

A therapist can provide a safe and supportive space for you to explore your emotions, gain insight into your behaviour and communication patterns, and develop coping strategies to navigate the challenges of relationship changes. Experiencing changes in relationships can indeed trigger feelings of hopelessness, but it is essential to remember that these feelings are temporary and can be navigated with support and self-care.

By allowing yourself to grieve, practising self-compassion, engaging in open communication, and seeking professional help, you can navigate relationship changes with resilience and develop a deeper understanding of yourself and your relationships. Remember that you are not alone in facing these challenges and that, with time and effort, you can find healing, growth, and a renewed sense of hope in your relationships.

Impact of Rejection

Rejection is a powerful and painful experience that can profoundly impact an individual's emotional well-being. Being faced with rejection, whether in the form of a failed relationship, job rejection, or social exclusion, can trigger feelings of hopelessness. Hopelessness is a state of mind characterised by a lack of optimism or belief in positive outcomes. One of the primary reasons why rejection can lead to feelings of hopelessness is the sense of loss and failure that often accompanies it.

When a person is rejected, they may feel like they have lost something important, whether it be a romantic partner, a job opportunity, or a sense of belonging within a social group. This loss can be excruciating and shake individuals' self-worth and confidence. Consequently, they may start to doubt their abilities and worth, creating a sense of hopelessness about their prospects. Rejection can also trigger feelings of isolation and loneliness, which may further exacerbate feelings of hopelessness.

When a person is rejected, they may feel alone in their pain and think that no one understands what they are going through. This sense of isolation can make it difficult for them to reach out for support and can deepen their feelings of hopelessness. Without a strong support system, individuals may struggle to see a way out of their current situation, leading to despair and hopelessness. Moreover, rejection can also fuel negative thought patterns and beliefs about oneself.

When a person experiences rejection, they may start to internalise the rejection as a reflection of their inadequacies or shortcomings. This negative self-talk can further erode their self-esteem and confidence, making it difficult for them to see a way forward. As a result, they may start believing they are unworthy of love, success, or happiness, leading to a deep hopelessness about their future.

However, it is essential to remember that rejection is not unusual and does not define one's worth or potential. Individuals must practise self-compassion and self-care during times of rejection to help them navigate feelings of hopelessness.

Seeking support from friends, family, or a therapist can also provide a safe space for individuals to process their emotions and gain a new perspective on their situation. Rejection can be a challenging and painful experience that can trigger feelings of hopelessness.

Individuals must recognise and validate their emotions during rejection while seeking support and practising self-care to help them navigate these complicated feelings. By acknowledging their emotions and taking steps to care for themselves, individuals can begin to heal from rejection and cultivate a sense of hope for the future.

Traumatic Experiences and Hopelessness
The Deep Impact of Trauma

Traumatic experiences have the power to profoundly affect individuals, often resulting in a range of emotional and psychological challenges. One of the most significant outcomes of trauma is the development of hopelessness. Events such as emotional or physical abuse, violence, accidents, or natural disasters can severely disrupt a person's sense of safety, control, and trust in the world. When someone endures trauma, their belief in the world as a secure and predictable place may be shattered. This loss of security can deeply undermine their trust in themselves and others. As individuals struggle to make sense of their experiences, they may feel increasingly disconnected from the world around them, leading to feelings of helplessness and hopelessness.

The aftermath of trauma can manifest in various ways, including anxiety, depression, post-traumatic stress disorder (PTSD), and complex emotional responses. Individuals may replay the traumatic event in their minds, experience vivid flashbacks, or avoid places and people that remind them of the trauma. The weight of these experiences can strain relationships, impact daily functioning, and diminish overall quality of life. Furthermore, the sense of isolation that often accompanies trauma can make it difficult for individuals to reach out for support, creating a cycle of suffering that feels impossible to break.

However, healing is possible. With the right support, individuals can begin to rebuild their sense of safety and trust. Professional help, such as therapy or counseling, can provide a safe space to process emotions and develop coping strategies. Support from loved ones, support groups, and community resources can also play a crucial role in the healing journey. By acknowledging the impact of trauma and seeking help, individuals can gradually regain control over their lives and rediscover a sense of hope and purpose. The path to recovery may be long and challenging, but with perseverance and support, it is possible to move forward and find healing. As individuals embark on the journey of healing, they may discover that rebuilding their sense of self and identity is crucial. Trauma can often leave people feeling defined by their experiences, but therapy and support can help them reclaim their narratives. By exploring their strengths, values, and passions, individuals can start to redefine who they are beyond the trauma. Moreover, fostering resilience is a key component of recovery. This can involve developing healthy coping mechanisms, practicing self-care, and cultivating a supportive network. Mindfulness practices, such as meditation or yoga, can also aid in managing stress and promoting emotional regulation. It's also important to recognize that healing is not a linear process. There may be setbacks and difficult days, but these are opportunities for growth and deeper understanding. By being patient and compassionate with themselves, individuals can navigate the complexities of their emotions and experiences.

Ultimately, healing from trauma is about finding ways to reclaim power and agency over one's life. It's about learning to trust again, not just others, but oneself. With time, support, and effort, individuals can transform their pain into a source of strength, emerging more resilient and hopeful than they ever thought possible. The journey may be unique for each person, but the potential for healing and growth is universal. By sharing stories, supporting one another, and seeking help, individuals can turn their traumatic experiences into a catalyst for personal transformation and empowerment.

Emotional Overwhelm and Negative Beliefs

Trauma often elicits intense emotions such as fear, anger, sadness, and guilt. These emotions can be overwhelming and difficult to manage, especially when they persist long after the traumatic event. The sense of being emotionally flooded can leave individuals feeling powerless and out of control. As a result, they may find it difficult to believe that things will ever improve, reinforcing a bleak outlook on life.

In many cases, trauma gives rise to persistent negative thoughts and beliefs. Individuals may begin to see themselves as weak, unworthy, or permanently damaged. They might also view the world as dangerous and feel powerless to protect themselves from future harm. These distorted beliefs can contribute significantly to feelings of hopelessness, as the person may see no escape from their emotional pain or suffering. These negative beliefs can become deeply ingrained, influencing various aspects of life, including relationships, work, and overall well-being. They may lead to self-sabotaging behaviors, strained relationships, and a pervasive sense of dissatisfaction. Challenging and reframing these beliefs is crucial for recovery. Therapeutic approaches like cognitive-behavioral therapy (CBT) can help individuals identify and challenge these negative thought patterns. By learning to recognize and dispute distorted beliefs, individuals can begin to develop a more balanced and compassionate view of themselves and the world.

Additionally, practices such as mindfulness, self-compassion, and gratitude can aid in shifting perspectives and fostering a more positive outlook. By cultivating a sense of self-awareness and self-acceptance, individuals can begin to break free from the grip of negative beliefs and emotions, paving the way for healing and growth. Ultimately, overcoming the negative impact of trauma requires patience, support, and a willingness to confront and challenge deeply ingrained beliefs. With the right tools and resources, individuals can learn to manage their emotions, develop resilience, and reclaim their lives. As individuals work to overcome the negative impact of trauma, they may also need to develop strategies for managing triggers and flashbacks. These can be intense and unpredictable, making everyday life challenging. However, with the right coping mechanisms, individuals can learn to navigate these difficult moments.

Building a support network is also crucial. Connecting with others who understand the impact of trauma can provide validation and a sense of community. Support groups, either in-person or online, can offer a safe space to share experiences and learn from others. Self-care is another essential aspect of recovery. Engaging in activities that bring joy and relaxation can help counterbalance the negative effects of trauma. This might include creative pursuits, exercise, or spending time in nature. Recovery from trauma is a unique and individual process. What works for one person may not work for another. It's essential to be patient and compassionate with oneself as you navigate this journey. Celebrate small victories, and don't hesitate to seek help when needed. Ultimately, healing from trauma is possible. With time, support, and the right tools, individuals can learn to manage their emotions, develop resilience, and reclaim their lives. By acknowledging the impact of trauma and seeking help, individuals can take the first steps towards a brighter, more hopeful future.

As individuals continue on their healing journey, they may also discover the importance of forgiveness and letting go. Forgiveness doesn't mean forgetting or condoning the traumatic experience, but rather releasing the emotional burden associated with it. This can be a powerful step towards healing, allowing individuals to break free from the past and move forward with greater ease. Letting go of the trauma's hold on one's life can also involve redefining personal boundaries and learning to prioritize one's own needs. By setting healthy limits and communicating effectively, individuals can regain a sense of control and agency over their lives.

Moreover, finding ways to honour and integrate the traumatic experience into one's narrative can be a meaningful way to heal. This might involve creative expression, such as writing, art, or music, or finding ways to help others who have experienced similar traumas.

By acknowledging the trauma's impact and working through the associated emotions, individuals can transform their experiences into opportunities for growth, resilience, and empowerment. This journey is not about erasing the past, but about reclaiming the present and shaping a more hopeful future.

Healing from trauma is a testament to the human spirit's capacity for resilience and transformation. With support, self-care, and a willingness to confront the past, individuals can emerge stronger, wiser, and more compassionate, ready to face whatever challenges come their way.

Isolation and Identity Loss

Another common consequence of trauma is isolation. Those who have experienced trauma often find it hard to connect with others. They may struggle to trust, feel like a burden, or fear being misunderstood. This disconnection can create a sense of loneliness and emotional detachment, which further deepens their hopelessness. When individuals feel that no one can relate to their pain or offer support, they may begin to believe that they must suffer in silence.

Trauma can also lead to a loss of identity and purpose. A person who once had clear goals, values, and a sense of self may feel lost or broken in the aftermath of trauma. This disruption of identity can make it difficult to envision a meaningful future. As hope for a better life fades, despair often takes its place. This loss of identity and purpose can manifest in various ways, such as feeling disconnected from activities that once brought joy, struggling to maintain relationships, or questioning one's values and beliefs. Trauma can shatter a person's sense of self, leaving them feeling fragmented and uncertain about their place in the world. Rebuilding a sense of identity and purpose is a crucial aspect of the healing process. This can involve exploring new interests, reconnecting with old passions, and rediscovering values and beliefs. Therapy, support groups, and creative expression can be valuable tools in this process. Moreover, reconnecting with others is essential in overcoming isolation. Building a supportive network of people who understand and validate one's experiences can help individuals feel seen, heard, and valued. This can involve seeking out support groups, online communities, or therapy groups specifically designed for trauma survivors. By slowly rebuilding connections with others and rediscovering a sense of purpose, individuals can begin to heal and find a new sense of meaning in life. This process takes time, patience, and compassion, but it is possible to emerge from trauma with a renewed sense of identity and hope for the future.

As individuals work to rebuild their sense of identity and purpose, they may also need to confront the ways in which trauma has impacted their relationships. Trauma can strain relationships with family and friends, leading to feelings of disconnection and isolation. However, with the right support and communication, relationships can also be a source of healing and strength. Learning to communicate effectively about one's needs and boundaries is crucial in rebuilding and maintaining healthy relationships. This can involve setting clear boundaries, practicing active listening, and expressing emotions in a healthy way.

Moreover, trauma can also impact one's sense of spirituality or connection to something greater than oneself. Some individuals may struggle with feelings of anger or disillusionment towards a higher power or the universe. Others may find comfort in their faith or spiritual practices. Exploring these feelings and finding ways to reconnect with one's spiritual self can be an important aspect of the healing journey.

Ultimately, healing from trauma is a journey that requires patience, compassion, and support. It's a process of rebuilding, rediscovering, and reconnecting with oneself and others. While the path may be challenging, many people find that they emerge from their experiences with a newfound sense of strength, resilience, and appreciation for life. By acknowledging the impact of trauma and seeking help, individuals can take the first steps towards healing and recovery. With time, support, and self-care, it's possible to transform the trauma into an opportunity for growth, healing, and a deeper understanding of oneself and the world.

As individuals continue on their healing journey, they may also discover the importance of self-compassion and self-forgiveness. Trauma can often leave people feeling guilty or ashamed, but practicing self-compassion can help alleviate these feelings. By treating themselves with kindness, understanding, and patience, individuals can begin to heal and move forward.

Additionally, finding ways to honor and acknowledge one's experiences can be a powerful way to process trauma. This might involve creating art, writing, or engaging in other creative activities that help express emotions and tell one's story. By giving voice to their experiences, individuals can begin to integrate their trauma into their narrative and find a sense of closure.

It's also important to recognize that healing from trauma is not a solo endeavour. Having a supportive network of people who understand and validate one's experiences can make a significant difference. Support groups, therapy, and online communities can provide a safe space to connect with others who have gone through similar experiences. Ultimately, healing from trauma is a journey of reclaiming one's life, identity, and sense of purpose. It's a process of transformation that requires courage, resilience, and support. By acknowledging the impact of trauma and seeking help, individuals can take the first steps towards healing and recovery. With time, patience, and support, it's possible to emerge from trauma with a newfound sense of strength, wisdom, and appreciation for life. The journey may be challenging, but the outcome can be incredibly rewarding, leading to a more authentic, meaningful, and fulfilling life.

Finding the Path to Healing

Despite the deep emotional toll of trauma, it is important to remember that healing is possible. Acknowledging the impact of trauma is the first step toward recovery. Individuals do not have to face their pain alone. Reaching out to trusted friends, family, or mental health professionals can offer vital support and guidance. Speaking about traumatic experiences in a safe, supportive environment can help individuals begin to process their emotions and regain a sense of agency.

In addition to professional help, engaging in self-care practices can support healing. Activities such as journaling, mindfulness, exercise, creative expression, or spending time in nature can help individuals reconnect with themselves and begin to restore their sense of well-being. These small but meaningful steps can foster resilience and help build a foundation for recovery. Healing from trauma is a unique and individual process, and what works for one person may not work for another. However, by acknowledging the impact of trauma and seeking support, individuals can begin to reclaim their lives and find a path towards healing.

Some key elements of the healing process include:

- Seeking professional help, such as therapy or counseling

- Building a support network of trusted friends, family, or support groups

- Practicing self-care, such as exercise, mindfulness, or creative activities

- Engaging in activities that promote relaxation and stress reduction

- Finding ways to process and express emotions, such as journaling or talking to a trusted friend or therapist.

By taking these steps, individuals can begin to heal and rebuild their lives. It's a journey that requires patience, compassion, and support, but with the right tools and resources, it's possible to emerge from trauma with a renewed sense of purpose and well-being. Ultimately, healing from trauma is about finding ways to reclaim power, rebuild resilience, and rediscover a sense of hope and purpose. It's a journey that can be challenging, but with the right support and resources, it's possible to create a brighter, more fulfilling future. As individuals progress on their healing journey, they may also discover the value of community and connection. Connecting with others who have experienced similar traumas can provide a sense of validation and understanding. Support groups, online forums, and group therapy can offer a safe space to share experiences, receive support, and learn from others. Moreover, finding ways to give back or make a positive impact can be a powerful way to heal. Engaging in volunteer work, advocacy, or creative pursuits can help individuals find meaning and purpose. By using their experiences to help others, individuals can transform their trauma into a source of strength and resilience.

Healing from trauma is not about erasing the past, but about reclaiming the present and shaping a more hopeful future. It's a journey that requires courage, patience, and support, but with the right tools and resources, individuals can emerge stronger, wiser, and more compassionate. By acknowledging the impact of trauma and seeking help, individuals can take the first steps towards healing and recovery. With time, support, and self-care, it's possible to create a brighter, more fulfilling future, and to find a sense of peace, purpose, and belonging.

As individuals continue to heal and grow, they may also discover new passions and interests. Engaging in activities that bring joy and fulfilment can help individuals reconnect with themselves and find a sense of purpose. Whether it's through creative pursuits, hobbies, or spending time in nature, finding activities that promote happiness and well-being can be a powerful way to support healing.

Moreover, learning to prioritize self-care and self-compassion is essential for maintaining emotional well-being. By treating themselves with kindness, understanding, and patience, individuals can develop a more positive and supportive relationship with themselves. Healing from trauma is a journey, not a destination. It's a process that requires effort, commitment, and support, but the rewards can be profound.

By acknowledging the impact of trauma and seeking help, individuals can take the first steps towards healing, growth, and transformation.

Ultimately, healing from trauma is about finding ways to reclaim power, rebuild resilience, and rediscover a sense of hope and purpose. It's a journey that can be challenging, but with the right support and resources, individuals can emerge stronger, wiser, and more compassionate, ready to face whatever challenges come their way.

Holding on to Hope

It is also crucial to remember that healing is not a linear process. Setbacks are a natural part of the journey, and individuals should be encouraged to treat themselves with patience and compassion as they work through their experiences. The path to recovery may be challenging, but with support, self-care, and perseverance, individuals can move from hopelessness toward a renewed sense of strength and purpose.

Trauma can be a life-altering experience, but it does not have to define a person's future. By recognising the profound impact of trauma and providing the support needed to address it, we can create a more compassionate and understanding environment for healing. There is always hope, even in the darkest moments, and with time and support, individuals can reclaim their lives and find peace after trauma. Holding onto hope is a vital part of the healing process. It's what helps individuals stay motivated, focused, and committed to their recovery. Hope can be a powerful catalyst for healing, and it's essential to nurture it throughout the journey. By acknowledging the complexities of trauma and the importance of support, we can create a more compassionate and understanding environment for healing. This can involve providing access to resources, such as therapy, support groups, and online communities, as well as promoting self-care and self-compassion. Ultimately, healing from trauma is possible, and it's never too late to start the journey. With patience, support, and perseverance, individuals can overcome the impact of trauma and find a renewed sense of purpose and meaning in life. By holding onto hope and staying committed to their recovery, individuals can reclaim their lives and find peace, healing, and happiness.

The journey of healing from trauma is unique to each individual, and it's essential to approach it with compassion, patience, and understanding. By acknowledging the impact of trauma and seeking support, individuals can take the first steps towards recovery. It's also important to recognize that healing is not a solo endeavour. Building a support network of trusted friends, family, or mental health professionals can provide a sense of safety and security. This network can offer emotional support, guidance, and validation, helping individuals navigate the complex process of healing.

As individuals progress on their healing journey, they may discover new strengths and resilience. They may learn to reframe their experiences, finding meaning and purpose in their struggles. By integrating their traumatic experiences into their narrative, individuals can reclaim their lives and find a sense of closure.

Healing from trauma is a testament to the human spirit's capacity for resilience, adaptability, and growth. It's a journey that requires courage, determination, and support, but the rewards can be profound. By holding onto hope and staying committed to their recovery, individuals can emerge stronger, wiser, and more compassionate, ready to face whatever challenges come their way.

In the end, healing from trauma is a testament to the human spirit's capacity for resilience and growth. It's a journey that requires courage, vulnerability, and support, but the rewards can be profound. By facing the pain of trauma head-on and seeking help, individuals can transform their experiences into opportunities for growth, healing, and self-discovery.

The Alcohol Mindset

Alcohol is a substance that profoundly affects individuals—not just physically but mentally, emotionally, and spiritually. For many, it begins as something harmless: a way to relax after a long day, unwind at social gatherings, or take the edge off life's stressors. In moderation, alcohol may seem manageable, even harmless. But what often starts casually can quietly evolve into something far more destructive. Over time, it can reshape how a person thinks, feels, and behaves—altering their perception of reality, their sense of self, and their ability to cope with life. This transformation marks the emergence of what I call the *alcohol mindset*—a mental and emotional framework in which alcohol becomes central to one's identity, routine, and coping mechanisms.

The alcohol mindset is not just about drinking frequently; it's about how deeply alcohol becomes embedded in a person's thinking. It is characterised by a persistent preoccupation with alcohol, a compulsive urge to drink, and a distorted understanding of alcohol's role in one's life. Individuals caught in this mindset often prioritise alcohol above responsibilities, relationships, and self-care. They may constantly think about when they'll have their next drink, how much they'll consume, or how to manage the aftereffects. Gradually, alcohol becomes the organising principle of life, pushing aside once-valued goals, passions, and people.

A particularly devastating aspect of this mindset is its deep link to hopelessness. For many individuals, alcohol use evolves into a means of emotional escape. It's not merely about having fun or fitting in—it becomes a way to numb pain, silence anxiety, or drown out trauma. It's a coping mechanism turned crutch. The temporary relief alcohol provides—those fleeting moments of calm or escape—are quickly replaced by the numbing weight of regret, confusion, and despair. As a depressant, alcohol disrupts the brain's chemistry, dampens emotional resilience, and intensifies the very suffering it's meant to soothe.

This emotional toll becomes increasingly apparent. Individuals often find that, when they are not drinking, life feels unbearably dull, empty, or unmanageable. Pleasure fades from previously enjoyed activities. Restlessness, irritability, or even panic sets in during sober periods. These symptoms reinforce the need to drink again—not for celebration, but for relief. Thus, the cycle continues.

Over time, alcohol dependency erodes not only one's health and happiness but also one's identity and sense of hope. The consequences—strained relationships, poor job performance, legal issues, declining physical health, and financial instability—accumulate, creating a heavy burden of shame, guilt, and self-loathing. Many believe they are broken, beyond help, incapable of real change. The more they try to suppress or hide the consequences, the deeper their isolation becomes.

The alcohol mindset also fosters tunnel vision. Life narrows. Days are structured around alcohol: acquiring it, consuming it, recovering from it, and concealing it. Activities that once brought joy or fulfilment now feel irrelevant or exhausting. Relationships suffer from neglect or repeated cycles of broken trust and unfulfilled promises. Support systems shrink as loved ones become distant, frustrated, or fearful. This isolation only magnifies despair and convinces the individual that no one could understand or help.

Physically, the consequences can be dire. Alcohol abuse damages vital organs like the liver and heart, impairs brain function, and increases the risk of chronic diseases. Cognitively, it blurs memory, slows decision-making, and impairs judgment. Emotionally, it fosters apathy, numbness, and detachment from both pain and joy. As the dependency deepens, even the desire to seek help can fade. Individuals feel trapped stuck in a cycle of drinking to escape the very despair that drinking helped create.

For some, alcohol becomes a substitute for connection. It replaces emotional vulnerability with artificial confidence, and intimate conversations with numb detachment. In times of stress, loneliness, or heartbreak, they turn to alcohol rather than to people. Over time, this erodes their ability to form meaningful relationships and weakens the emotional tools needed to face life without a substance buffer.

Financial consequences often follow. Alcohol can be an expensive habit, especially when it becomes daily or excessive. As priorities shift, individuals may find themselves sacrificing essentials—rent, food, healthcare—in order to maintain their access to alcohol. Financial instability only adds to the burden of stress and shame, reinforcing feelings of helplessness.

And yet, in the darkest depths of this mindset, there remains a glimmer of hope—though it may be buried under years of pain and denial. Recovery is not only possible, but entirely within reach. The first step is awareness: recognising how alcohol has shaped one's life, thoughts, and choices. Understanding the alcohol mindset does not mean accepting it as permanent. Rather, it's a way of seeing clearly—of naming the problem so that it can be faced.

Breaking free requires courage, commitment, and support. There is no single path to healing, but there are many effective ones: therapy, counselling, rehabilitation programs, support groups, and sober communities. These offer structure, accountability, and—perhaps most importantly—hope. Recovery isn't just about abstaining from alcohol. It's about learning new ways to cope with pain, rediscovering purpose, rebuilding trust, and restoring emotional connection.

Healing from the alcohol mindset is a journey of transformation. It means reclaiming life: not the life you had before addiction, but a new one—stronger, more honest, and rooted in true self-worth. It's about recognising that your past does not define your future. That you are capable of change. That you are not alone.

The alcohol mindset is powerful, but it is not invincible. No matter how far someone has fallen into addiction's grip, the road to healing is still open. With the right tools, the right support, and a willingness to face the truth, a meaningful and fulfilling life—free from the cycle of despair—is entirely possible.

Drug Abuse

Drug abuse is a pervasive problem that affects individuals, families, and communities worldwide. The use of drugs not only has physical and mental health consequences but also leads to profound social and emotional impacts. One of the most devastating consequences of drug use is the sense of hopelessness that it can engender in individuals. The use of drugs alters brain chemistry and can disrupt the brain's reward system, leading to a cycle of dependence and cravings.

As individuals become more dependent on drugs, they may experience a sense of hopelessness as they struggle to break free from the grip of addiction.

The psychological impact of drug abuse can be overwhelming, leading individuals to feel trapped in a cycle of self-destructive behaviour with no way out. The social effects of drug abuse can also contribute to feelings of hopelessness.

Drug addiction can strain relationships with family and friends, leading to feelings of isolation and detachment. Individuals who are struggling with drug abuse may find it challenging to maintain employment or housing, thereby further exacerbating their sense of hopelessness.

The stigma associated with drug addiction can also contribute to feelings of shame and worthlessness, making it even harder for individuals to seek help and support. The economic consequences of drug abuse can further compound feelings of hopelessness. Individuals who are addicted to drugs may struggle to hold down a job or may engage in criminal behaviour to support their habit.

This can lead to financial instability and poverty, further reinforcing feelings of hopelessness and despair. The economic impact of drug abuse can create a cycle of poverty and addiction that is difficult to break, trapping individuals in a cycle of hopelessness and despair.

Lack of Education

Education is widely recognised as a fundamental tool for personal and societal development. It equips individuals with the knowledge, skills, and opportunities necessary to lead fulfilling lives and contribute positively to society. However, when individuals lack access to quality education or cannot complete it, it can profoundly affect their hope and optimism. One of the primary ways a lack of education can contribute to hopelessness is through limited social mobility. Education is often seen as a pathway to social and economic advancement, as it provides individuals with the skills and qualifications needed to secure better job opportunities and higher incomes. Without access to education, individuals may find themselves trapped in cycles of poverty and limited opportunities, leading to feelings of hopelessness about their prospects.

Additionally, a lack of education can impact social relationships, as individuals may feel isolated or marginalised due to their limited knowledge and skills. The economic consequences of a lack of education can also contribute to feelings of hopelessness. Individuals with low levels of education are more likely to face unemployment, underemployment, and lower wages than their more educated counterparts. This can lead to financial insecurity, limited resource access, and powerlessness about one's economic future.

A lack of education can create barriers to economic mobility and success, reinforcing hopelessness and despair among individuals unable to access quality education. The psychological impact of a lack of education on hopelessness is significant. Education provides individuals with knowledge and skills and fosters critical thinking, problem-solving abilities, and a sense of self-efficacy. Without access to education, individuals may struggle to develop these essential skills and feel ill-equipped to navigate life's challenges. This can lead to feelings of inadequacy, low self-esteem, and a lack of confidence in one's abilities, all of which can contribute to feelings of hopelessness about one's future.

A lack of education can affect individuals' hope and optimism. Socially, economically, and psychologically, the absence of education can create barriers to success and opportunities, leading to feelings of hopelessness and despair. Society needs to prioritise education as a fundamental human right and invest in programmes and initiatives that ensure access to quality education for all individuals. By addressing the root causes of educational deprivation and providing support for those who lack access to education, we can help individuals overcome feelings of hopelessness and build brighter futures for themselves and their communities.

Lack of Trust

Trust is fundamental to human relationships as the foundation for connection, cooperation, and mutual understanding. When trust is broken, however, the consequences can be devastating, leading to feelings of betrayal, disillusionment, and hopelessness. The psychological impact of broken trust can be profound. Trust is closely linked to feelings of security, safety, and predictability in relationships. When trust is betrayed, individuals may experience various negative emotions, including anger, sadness, and confusion.

Loss of trust can shatter individuals' sense of reality and stability, leading to feelings of vulnerability and insecurity. This can create a sense of hopelessness as individuals struggle to make sense of their experiences and navigate the uncertainty of broken trust. The emotional consequences of broken trust can also contribute to feelings of hopelessness. Trust is often associated with closeness, intimacy, and connection with others.

When trust is violated, individuals may experience a sense of emotional distance, isolation, and disconnection from those they once trusted. This can lead to loneliness, sadness, and despair as individuals grapple with the aftermath of betrayal.

The emotional toll of broken trust can be overwhelming, leaving individuals feeling lost and adrift in a sea of uncertainty and doubt. The erosion of trust can have significant social implications, impacting individuals' relationships and sense of community. Trust is essential for building and maintaining healthy, supportive relationships with others. When trust is broken, individuals may struggle to trust others, leading to feelings of isolation and detachment. This can create a sense of hopelessness as individuals feel disconnected from their social networks and cannot rely on others for support and understanding.

The breakdown of trust can erode the fabric of communities, leading to feelings of distrust, suspicion, and division among individuals. Betrayal of trust can have far-reaching consequences on individuals' hope and optimism.

Psychologically, emotionally, and socially, broken trust can lead to feelings of vulnerability, disconnection, and despair. Individuals in such circumstances must rebuild trust in themselves and others, even in the face of betrayal. By fostering open communication, empathy, and forgiveness, individuals can begin to heal from the wounds of broken trust and cultivate a sense of hope and resilience in the face of adversity.

Lack of Belief

Belief is a powerful force that shapes our perceptions, attitudes, and behaviours. It gives individuals a sense of purpose, meaning, and direction. When individuals lack belief in themselves, others, or the world around them, it can lead to hopelessness and despair. The psychological impact of lacking belief can be significant.

Belief is a guiding force that shapes individuals' thoughts, decisions, and actions. When individuals lack belief in themselves or their abilities, they may experience self-doubt, inadequacy, and worthlessness. This can lead to a negative self-perception and a lack of confidence to overcome challenges and achieve goals. The absence of belief can create a sense of hopelessness as individuals struggle to find meaning and purpose. The emotional consequences of lacking belief can also contribute to feelings of hopelessness.

Belief is often associated with positive emotions such as optimism, confidence, and resilience. When individuals lack belief, they may experience a range of negative emotions, including fear, anxiety, and depression. These emotions can weigh heavily on individuals, leading to despair and helplessness about their ability to cope with life's challenges.

The absence of belief can create a sense of emotional emptiness and disconnection from oneself and others, further exacerbating feelings of hopelessness.

A lack of belief can also have social implications, impacting individuals' relationships and sense of belonging. Belief in others and the world is essential for building trust, connection, and cooperation. Individuals lacking belief in others may struggle to form meaningful relationships and feel isolated or alienated from their social networks. This can lead to feelings of loneliness, disconnection, and hopelessness as individuals navigate the challenges of interpersonal relationships without a foundation of belief.

The absence of belief can profoundly affect individuals' hope and optimism. Psychologically, emotionally, and socially, lacking belief can lead to feelings of self-doubt, emotional distress, and social isolation. Individuals need to cultivate belief in themselves, others, and the world around them to overcome feelings of hopelessness and despair. By fostering a sense of belief and resilience, individuals can navigate life's challenges with confidence, purpose, and hope for the future.

Lack of Confidence

Confidence is crucial to an individual's ability to navigate challenges, pursue goals, and maintain a positive outlook on life. When individuals lack confidence in themselves, their abilities, or their prospects, it can lead to hopelessness and despair. The psychological impact of lacking confidence can be profound.

Confidence is closely tied to self-esteem and self-efficacy, influencing how individuals perceive themselves and their capabilities. Individuals lacking confidence may experience self-doubt, insecurity, and inadequacy. This can lead to a negative self-perception and a sense of powerlessness in the face of challenges. The absence of confidence can create a cycle of self-defeating thoughts and behaviours, contributing to hopelessness as individuals struggle to believe in their ability to overcome obstacles and achieve their goals.

The emotional consequences of lacking confidence can also contribute to feelings of hopelessness. Confidence is often associated with positive emotions such as optimism, resilience, and self-assurance. When individuals lack confidence, they may experience a range of negative emotions, including anxiety, fear, and depression. These emotions can erode individuals' well-being and stability, leading to despair and helplessness about coping with life's challenges. The absence of confidence can create a barrier to emotional growth and resilience, further reinforcing feelings of hopelessness and inadequacy.

A lack of confidence can also have social implications, impacting individuals' relationships and sense of belonging. Confidence is essential for building and maintaining healthy, supportive relationships with others. When individuals lack confidence, they may struggle to assert themselves, communicate effectively, and form meaningful connections with others. This can lead to feelings of isolation, loneliness, and disconnection from social networks, further exacerbating feelings of hopelessness and despair as individuals attempt to navigate interpersonal relationships without a sense of confidence and self-assurance. The absence of confidence can have far-reaching effects on individuals' sense of hope and optimism.

Psychologically, emotionally, and socially, lacking confidence can lead to feelings of self-doubt, emotional distress, and social isolation. Individuals need to build their confidence and self-belief to overcome feelings of hopelessness and cultivate a sense of empowerment and resilience. By fostering confidence in themselves and their abilities, individuals can approach challenges positively, navigate relationships with assertiveness and empathy, and maintain hope for a brighter future.

Lack of Motivation

Motivation is the driving force that propels individuals towards their goals and aspirations. It serves as the spark that ignites passion and determination, leading individuals to act and strive for success. However, when they lack motivation, individuals may be trapped in a cycle of hopelessness and despair. Lack of motivation can create a vicious cycle that is difficult to break. When individuals lack the drive to pursue their goals, they may procrastinate, make excuses, or avoid acting altogether. This can lead to feelings of inadequacy, self-doubt, and feeling stuck in a rut.

As a result, individuals may experience a downward spiral of negative emotions and thoughts, further diminishing their motivation and perpetuating the cycle of hopelessness. One of the most significant consequences of a lack of motivation is its impact on mental health. When individuals lack the drive to pursue their goals and dreams, they may experience feelings of worthlessness, low self-esteem, and depression. These negative emotions can take a toll on their mental well-being, leading to a sense of hopelessness and despair. Over time, this can result in a downward spiral of mental health issues, making it even more challenging for individuals to find the motivation to break free from the cycle of hopelessness.

Another consequence of a lack of motivation is the strain it can place on relationships. When individuals are unmotivated, they may struggle to engage with others, fulfil their responsibilities, or participate in social activities. This can lead to feelings of isolation, loneliness, and disconnection from loved ones. As a result, relationships may suffer, further exacerbating feelings of hopelessness and despair. A lack of motivation can also result in missed personal and professional growth opportunities. When individuals lack the drive to pursue their goals, they may miss chances to advance their careers, learn new skills, or experience personal fulfilment. This can lead to regret and dissatisfaction, further deepening hopelessness and despair.

The consequences of a lack of motivation can be far-reaching; if they can recognise the detrimental effects of this lack of drive and take proactive steps to reignite their motivation, individuals can break free from the cycle of hopelessness and move towards a more fulfilling and purposeful life. It is essential to remember that even in the darkest moments, a glimmer of hope is always waiting to be discovered.

Chronic Stress

Chronic stress is a pervasive and insidious condition that affects millions of individuals worldwide. It occurs when an individual is exposed to prolonged periods of stress without adequate relief or coping mechanisms. While stress is a natural response to challenging situations, chronic stress can have profound implications for both physical and mental health. One of the primary causes of chronic stress is ongoing exposure to demanding or overwhelming situations. This can include work-related pressures, financial difficulties, relationship problems, or health issues.

When individuals are unable to manage or mitigate these stressors effectively, they may find themselves trapped in a cycle of chronic stress that can have far-reaching consequences. Furthermore, chronic stress can also be exacerbated by internal factors such as perfectionism, negative self-talk, or unrealistic expectations. Individuals who place high demands on themselves or who struggle with self-compassion may be more susceptible to chronic stress. Additionally, personality traits such as Type A behaviour, which is characterised by competitiveness and a sense of urgency, can also contribute to chronic stress.

The effects of chronic stress on both physical and mental health are profound. Prolonged exposure to stress hormones such as cortisol can lead to a range of physical health problems, including cardiovascular issues, digestive disorders, and weakened immune function.

Chronic stress is also linked to mental health conditions such as anxiety, depression, and burnout. Over time, chronic stress can significantly affect an individual's overall well-being and quality of life. Fortunately, there are strategies that individuals can employ to manage and reduce chronic stress. These include stress management techniques such as mindfulness, relaxation exercises, and deep breathing. Regular physical activity, adequate sleep, and a healthy diet can also help mitigate the effects of chronic stress on the body.

Additionally, seeking support from friends, family, or mental health professionals can provide valuable resources for coping with chronic stress. Chronic stress is a pervasive condition that can have profound implications for both physical and psychological health. Understanding the causes and effects of chronic stress is essential for developing effective strategies for managing this condition. By implementing stress management techniques, seeking support, and prioritising self-care, individuals can take proactive steps to reduce the impact of chronic stress on their well-being.

Mental Health Disorders

Mental health disorders affect a person's thinking, feelings, behaviour, or mood. These disorders can significantly impact an individual's daily life, relationships, and well-being. Mental health disorders are more common than many people realise, with millions of individuals worldwide experiencing these conditions. They can manifest in various forms, including anxiety disorders, mood disorders (such as depression and bipolar disorder), psychotic disorders (such as schizophrenia), eating disorders, and personality disorders, among others. These disorders can be caused by genetic, biological, environmental, or psychological factors.

Genetic predisposition plays a significant role in the development of mental health disorders, as individuals with a family history of certain conditions may be more likely to experience them themselves.

Biological factors, such as imbalances in neurotransmitters or brain chemistry, can also contribute to the onset of mental health disorders. Environmental factors, such as trauma, abuse, stress, or substance abuse, can further increase the risk of developing a mental health disorder.

The effects of mental health disorders can be wide-ranging and profound. Individuals with these conditions may experience symptoms such as persistent sadness, anxiety, irritability, mood swings, changes in appetite or sleep patterns, social withdrawal, hallucinations, delusions, or self-harm behaviours.

These symptoms can significantly impact a person's ability to function daily, maintain relationships, or perform at work or school. Treatment options for mental health disorders vary depending on the specific condition and its severity. Common approaches include psychotherapy (such as cognitive-behavioural therapy or talk therapy), medication (such as antidepressants or antipsychotics), lifestyle changes (such as exercise, nutrition, and stress management), and support groups. In some cases, combining these approaches may be necessary to manage symptoms and improve overall well-being effectively. It is essential to recognise that mental health disorders are legitimate medical conditions that require proper diagnosis and treatment.

Seeking help from a mental health professional, such as a psychologist, psychiatrist, or counsellor, is crucial for individuals experiencing symptoms of a mental health disorder. With the proper support and treatment, individuals can learn to manage their symptoms, improve their quality of life, and work towards recovery. Mental health disorders are common conditions that can have a significant impact on an individual's life.

Understanding the causes, effects, and treatment options for these disorders is essential for promoting mental health awareness and reducing stigma. By seeking help, accessing appropriate treatment, and building a support network, individuals can effectively manage their mental health and work towards a brighter future.

Lack of Support

Lack of support is a significant and often overlooked cause of hopelessness in individuals. Human beings are social creatures who thrive on connection, empathy, and understanding from others. When individuals do not have a strong support system, they may feel isolated, misunderstood, or overwhelmed by life's challenges.

One of the primary ways in which lack of support can lead to hopelessness is through feelings of loneliness and isolation. When individuals do not have people they can turn to for emotional support, encouragement, or guidance, they may feel as if they are facing their struggles alone. This sense of isolation can intensify negative emotions and make it difficult for individuals to see a way out of their difficulties, leading to a deepening sense of hopelessness.

Moreover, the absence of a support system can also impact an individual's sense of self-worth and belonging. When people do not have others who validate their experiences, offer reassurance, or provide a sense of belonging, they may doubt their value and worthiness. This lack of validation and affirmation can contribute to feelings of inadequacy, self-doubt, and hopelessness.

Additionally, without a support system, individuals may struggle to cope with life's challenges and setbacks. Supportive relationships can offer a buffer against stress, provide different perspectives on problems, and help individuals navigate difficult situations.

When individuals lack this kind of support, they may feel overwhelmed by their circumstances and are unsure how to move forward, increasing hopelessness and despair. Building a support network is essential for combating feelings of hopelessness and fostering resilience in the face of adversity.

A support network can consist of friends, family members, mentors, therapists, support groups, or others who provide emotional support, practical assistance, and a listening ear. By reaching out to others, sharing their struggles, and seeking help, individuals can break free from hopelessness and find renewed strength and hope.

Lack of support is a significant cause of hopelessness that can have profound effects on an individual's mental health and well-being. Recognising the importance of building a support network and seeking help when needed is crucial for overcoming feelings of isolation, self-doubt, and despair. By fostering connections with others, individuals can find the support and encouragement they need to navigate life's challenges, build resilience, and cultivate a sense of hope for the future.

Forms of Hopelessness
Detachment

Detachment is a concept that is often associated with feelings of isolation, estrangement, and disconnection from society. It occurs when an individual feels separated or disconnected from the world around them, leading to a sense of hopelessness and despair. Detachment can manifest in many forms, including social, economic, and psychological isolation. Social Detachment occurs when an individual feels disconnected from their community or social group, leading to loneliness and isolation. On the other hand, Economic Detachment occurs when an individual feels disconnected from their work or the financial system, leading to feelings of powerlessness and disenfranchisement.

Finally, Psychological Detachment occurs when an individual feels disconnected from their thoughts and emotions, leading to feelings of confusion and disorientation. One of the leading causes of detachment is the breakdown of social bonds and relationships. In our modern society, individuals are often encouraged to focus on individual success and achievement, thus leading to a sense of competition and isolation. This focus on individualism can result in a lack of strong social ties and relationships, leading to feelings of detachment and disconnection.

Another cause of detachment is the dehumanising effects of capitalism. In a capitalist society, individuals are often treated as commodities or resources to be exploited for profit. This can lead to powerlessness and disenfranchisement as individuals feel disconnected from their work and sense of agency.

Furthermore, the rapid rise of technology has also contributed to feelings of detachment. In our digital age, individuals are often more connected to their devices than to each other, leading to disconnection and isolation. Social media can exacerbate feelings of detachment, as individuals compare themselves to others and sometimes feel inadequate or left out. The consequences of detachment can be severe and far-reaching.

Individuals who think they are alienated often experience feelings of hopelessness, despair, and apathy. They may struggle to form meaningful relationships or find fulfilment in their work, leading to a sense of emptiness and disconnection.

Detachment can also lead to mental health issues such as depression and anxiety, further exacerbating feelings of hopelessness and despair.

In addition, Detachment can also have negative consequences for society. Social cohesion and solidarity can break down when individuals feel disconnected from each other and their communities. This can lead to increased social unrest, conflict, and division, further perpetuating feelings of hopelessness and despair.

Despite the negative consequences of detachment, there is still hope for those who feel disconnected and isolated. One solution is to focus on building strong social bonds and relationships. Individuals can combat feelings of detachment and find a sense of belonging and connection by connecting with others and forming meaningful relationships.

Another solution is to cultivate a sense of purpose and meaning in life. By finding activities or causes that are meaningful and fulfilling, individuals can overcome feelings of hopelessness and despair. This might involve pursuing hobbies, volunteering, or engaging in creative pursuits that bring joy and fulfilment.

Furthermore, individuals must practise self-care and prioritise their mental and emotional well-being. By caring for themselves and seeking support when needed, individuals can cope better with feelings of detachment and hopelessness. Detachment is a form of hopelessness that can have severe consequences for individuals and society.

By understanding the causes and consequences of detachment, we can work towards finding solutions to combat feelings of disconnection and despair. By building strong social bonds, finding purpose and meaning in life, and prioritising self-care, individuals can overcome feelings of detachment and find hope and fulfilment.

Forsakenness

In a world filled with constant change and unpredictability, it is common for individuals to experience moments of feeling forsaken. This sense of abandonment or neglect can arise from various circumstances, such as losing a loved one, betraying a friend, or even feeling overlooked or unappreciated. Forsakenness can manifest itself in diverse ways, but one common thread that ties these experiences together is the overwhelming sense of hopelessness that accompanies them.

When someone feels forsaken, they often feel as though they are alone in the world, with no one to turn to for support or guidance. This can lead to a deep feeling of despair and helplessness, as though there is no way out of the situation they find themselves in. This hopelessness can suffocate a person, making it difficult for individuals to see beyond their current circumstances and envision a better future.

One of the key reasons why forsakenness can lead to hopelessness is the perception that one's worth or value is tied to the actions or opinions of others. When people feel abandoned or neglected by people they care about, it is sometimes easier to internalise these feelings and believe that they are unworthy of love or support from others. This can create a cycle of self-doubt and self-criticism, thus further fuelling the hopelessness that accompanies forsakenness.

Additionally, forsakenness can stem from loss or betrayal, shattering one's sense of trust and security. When someone feels abandoned by a loved one or betrayed by a friend, it may not be easy to rebuild that trust and form meaningful connections. This can lead to feelings of isolation and loneliness, further exacerbating the sense of hopelessness that comes with forsakenness.

Furthermore, forsakenness can also be compounded by external factors, such as societal expectations or cultural norms. In a society that places a high value on success and achievement, those who feel abandoned or neglected may struggle to meet these standards, leading to feelings of inadequacy or failure. This can create a sense of hopelessness, as individuals may feel they will never be able to meet the expectations placed upon them.

To overcome the sense of hopelessness that comes with forsakenness, individuals need to recognise that their worth and value are not dependent on the actions or opinions of others. It is essential to cultivate a sense of self-worth and self-compassion and to recognise that everyone experiences moments of forsakenness at some point in their lives. By acknowledging and accepting these feelings, individuals can begin to heal and move forward, knowing they are not alone in their struggles.

Additionally, seeking support from others can be crucial for overcoming one's sense of forsakenness and hopelessness. Whether through therapy, support groups or reaching out to friends and loved ones, connecting with others and sharing one's feelings in a safe and supportive environment is essential. By opening up and allowing themselves to be vulnerable, individuals can rebuild trust and form meaningful connections, finding hope and belonging.

Forsakenness is a form of hopelessness that can be deeply painful and isolating. However, it is essential to remember that these feelings are temporary, and there is always hope for a brighter future. By cultivating self-worth, seeking support from others, and acknowledging one's emotions, individuals can heal and move forward, knowing they are not alone in their struggles. Hopelessness may feel overwhelming in moments of forsakenness, but with time and self-reflection, it is possible to regain hope and purpose.

Lack of Inspiration

Inspiration is often described as the driving force behind creativity, motivation, and achievement. It fuels us to pursue our dreams, overcome obstacles, and bring our ideas to life. However, when we lack inspiration, we can feel lost, unmotivated, and hopeless. When we lack inspiration, it can feel like we are stuck in a rut, unable to see a way forward or find the motivation to act. This feeling of stagnation can lead to a sense of hopelessness, where we doubt our abilities, lose faith in ourselves, and wonder if we will ever be able to achieve our goals.

Without inspiration, we may find it challenging to muster the energy or enthusiasm needed to make progress and may even begin to question the value of our pursuits. One of the key reasons why lack of inspiration can lead to hopelessness is that inspiration is intricately linked to our sense of purpose and meaning in life. When we are inspired, we feel a deep connection to our passions, values, and aspirations and are driven by a sense of purpose that gives our lives direction and meaning. However, when we lack inspiration, we may lose sight of this sense of purpose and find ourselves adrift in a sea of uncertainty and doubt.

Another reason a lack of inspiration can lead to hopelessness is that inspiration is often fuelled by positive emotions such as joy, excitement, and passion. When we are inspired, we feel a sense of exhilaration and enthusiasm that propels us forward and gives us the energy to tackle challenges and overcome obstacles. However, when we lack inspiration, we may feel flat, disinterested, and apathetic, making it difficult to summon the motivation needed to keep going. In addition, lack of inspiration can also be exacerbated by external factors such as stress, burnout, and lack of support.

Finding the mental space and emotional energy needed to tap into our creative and motivational reserves can be difficult when we are pressured or overwhelmed by our responsibilities. Likewise, when we lack the encouragement and validation of others, it can be hard to believe in ourselves and our abilities, thus making it even harder to find inspiration and hope.

So, how can we overcome the challenges of lack of inspiration and find a way out of hopelessness? One strategy is to focus on self-care and well-being, taking time to rest, recharge, and nurture ourselves physically and mentally.

By prioritising our needs and finding ways to reduce stress and anxiety, we can create conditions for inspiration to flourish and hope to be restored. Another strategy is to seek out sources of inspiration in our environment, such as nature, art, music, and literature. By immersing ourselves in the beauty and creativity surrounding us, we can open ourselves up to innovative ideas, perspectives, and possibilities by reigniting our passion and motivation. Additionally, connecting with others who share our passions and aspirations can give us the encouragement, support, and inspiration to keep going, even when the going gets tough.

Lack of inspiration can be a form of hopelessness, leaving us feeling stuck, discouraged, and unsure of our path. However, by understanding the relationship between inspiration and hope and by taking steps to nurture our creativity, motivation, and well-being, we can overcome the challenges of lack of inspiration and find a way out of hopelessness.

By staying connected to our sense of purpose, seeking out sources of inspiration, and drawing on the support of others, we can reignite our passion, restore our motivation, and reclaim our hope for a brighter future.

Powerlessness

Powerlessness is a feeling that many of us have experienced at some point in our lives. It is the sense that we have no control over our circumstances and are at the mercy of forces beyond our control. This feeling of powerlessness can be overwhelming and can lead to a sense of hopelessness. When we feel powerless, we may find it difficult to see a way out of our situation and think there is no hope for the future. Powerlessness can take many different forms. It can manifest in relationships where we cannot assert ourselves or stand up for our needs. It can appear in the workplace, where we may feel trapped in an unfulfilling or abusive job. It can also show up in larger societal issues, where we may feel powerless to effect change in the face of injustice or oppression.

One of the key ways in which powerlessness can lead to hopelessness is through a sense of resignation. When we feel that we have no control over our circumstances, we may start to believe that things will never change. This belief can be incredibly demoralising and can sap our motivation to take action to improve our situation. In relationships, for example, powerlessness can lead to hopelessness when we believe that our partner will never change or that the relationship dynamics will never improve.

This belief can prevent us from taking steps to address the issues in the relationship, leading to a cycle of powerlessness and hopelessness. In the workplace, powerlessness can lead to hopelessness when we believe that there is no way out of a toxic work environment or that we will never be able to find a more fulfilling job. This belief can lead to a sense of resignation, where we stop looking for opportunities to improve our situation and instead accept our circumstances.

On a larger scale, powerlessness can lead to hopelessness when we feel there is nothing we can do to address societal issues such as inequality, climate change, or political corruption. This sense of powerlessness can prevent us from acting to effect change, leading to a feeling of despair and hopelessness about the future.

However, it is essential to remember that powerlessness is different from hopelessness. While powerlessness may make us feel like we have no control over our circumstances, there is always the possibility of change. By recognising how powerlessness can lead to hopelessness, we can break out of this cycle and regain a sense of agency in our lives.

One way to combat the hopelessness that can arise from powerlessness is to focus on what we can control. While there may be many aspects of our circumstances that are beyond our control, there are always things that we can do to improve our situation. By taking small steps to assert ourselves in relationships, advocate for us in the workplace, or get involved in social causes that matter to us, we can start to build a sense of agency and empowerment.

Another way to combat hopelessness in the face of powerlessness is to seek support from others. Talking to friends, family members, or a therapist can help us gain perspective on our situation and find new ways of approaching our challenges. By sharing our feelings of powerlessness with others, we can begin to see that we are not alone in our struggles and that there are people who care about us and want to help us find a way forward.

Powerlessness is not a permanent state. While it may feel overwhelming, change and growth are always possible. By recognising how powerlessness can contribute to feelings of hopelessness, we can break out of this cycle and reclaim our sense of agency and empowerment. Through small steps and the support of others, we can build a sense of hope for the future, even in the face of challenging circumstances.

Oppression

Oppression, in its many forms, has long been recognised as a powerful force that stifles individual agency and autonomy. It can manifest in many ways, from social and economic inequality to political repression and discrimination. However, one of the most insidious aspects of oppression is the way it breeds a sense of hopelessness among those who experience it.

When people are constantly marginalised and denied fundamental rights and opportunities, it can be difficult to imagine a future where they can live freely and fulfil their potential. One of the key ways in which oppression breeds hopelessness is by stripping individuals of their sense of agency and control over their own lives. When people are denied fundamental rights and freedoms, such as the right to education, healthcare, or fair treatment under the law, it may be too easy and tempting to feel powerless and helpless and give up in the face of systemic injustices.

This sense of powerlessness can be particularly acute for marginalised groups, such as racial or ethnic minorities, women, LGBTQ+ individuals, and people with disabilities, who may face multiple forms of oppression simultaneously. Moreover, oppression can also create a pervasive sense of despair by limiting individuals' access to opportunities for social and economic advancement.

For example, when people are discriminated against in the job market, denied access to quality education, or subjected to violence and harassment, it may be difficult for them to envision a future in which they can achieve their goals and aspirations.

This lack of hope can be especially damaging for young people, who may grow up in environments where they are constantly told that their dreams are unattainable because, in addition to these external forms of oppression, individuals who experience ongoing discrimination and marginalisation may also internalise feelings of hopelessness and self-doubt.

This internalised oppression can manifest in a variety of ways, from low self-esteem and self-blame to feelings of worthlessness and vulnerability.

When people are constantly told that they are inferior or unworthy because of their identities, it can be difficult for them to shake off these harmful beliefs and develop a sense of self-worth and confidence. However, while oppression can create a deep sense of hopelessness, it is essential to recognise that there are also ways to resist and overcome it.

One of the most powerful tools for combating oppression is collective action and solidarity. When individuals come together to challenge unjust systems and advocate for their rights, they can build a sense of community and empowerment that can help counteract feelings of hopelessness and despair.

Marginalised groups can demonstrate their strength and resilience in the face of adversity by organising protests, strikes, and other forms of resistance. Furthermore, education and awareness can also be powerful tools for challenging oppression and fostering hope among those who experience it.

By learning about the history of oppression and understanding how it operates in society, individuals can develop a critical consciousness that allows them to identify and resist injustice.

Moreover, when people are given opportunities to learn and grow, they can develop the skills and knowledge they need to advocate for themselves and others and create a more just and equitable world. Although oppression can create a deep sense of hopelessness among individuals and communities, it is essential to remember that there are always ways to resist and overcome it.

By building solidarity, educating ourselves and others, and advocating for our rights, we can create a more just and equitable society where all individuals can thrive and fulfil their potential. Hope should not be extinguished in the face of oppression. It is the fuel that drives us to keep fighting for a better future concerning issues of race, gender, sexual orientation, or socioeconomic status.

Limitedness

Hope is a powerful force that can drive us forward, even in adversity. It is the belief that better things are possible and that there is light at the end of the tunnel. Hope gives us the strength to keep going when things get tough; consequently, we believe tomorrow will be better. However, when we are confronted with limitations that seem insurmountable, hope can quickly turn into hopelessness.

Limitedness, or being constrained or restricted somehow, can be a significant source of hopelessness. When we feel that our options are limited and that there is no way out of our current situation, it may be easy to lose hope. Limitedness can take many forms - limited financial resources, limited opportunities for advancement, limited physical abilities - but no matter the source, the result is often a sense of hopelessness.

One way limitedness can lead to hopelessness is through a feeling of powerlessness. When faced with circumstances we cannot control, it may be challenging to see a way out. We may feel trapped and unable to change our situation, which can quickly lead to a sense of hopelessness.

This feeling of powerlessness can be particularly acute when our limitations are imposed by external forces beyond our control, such as systemic barriers or societal norms. Limitedness can also lead to hopelessness by limiting our sense of possibility. When faced with insurmountable constraints, it may be hard to imagine a better future. We may feel stuck in our current situation and unable to see any way out. This lack of vision can quickly turn into hopelessness as we struggle to find a way forward in the face of our limitations.

Limitedness can also erode our sense of self-worth, leading to feelings of hopelessness. We may be driven to start questioning our values when we are constantly reminded of our limitations, whether due to external circumstances or internal beliefs. We may begin to doubt our abilities and worth, creating hopelessness about our prospects. This lack of self-esteem can be a significant barrier to finding hope in the face of limitedness.

Despite limited challenges, it is essential to remember that hope is not necessarily tied to the absence of limitations. Even in the face of constraints, hope can still exist. It might look different at that time than the hope we feel in more ideal circumstances, but it is no less powerful.

One way to find hope in the face of limitedness is to focus on what is within our control. While there may be external forces that are limiting our options, there are often different choices that we can make. By focusing on the things we can change rather than those beyond our control, we can maintain a sense of agency and hope in the face of limitedness.

Another way to cultivate hope in the face of limitedness is to seek out support from others. When we feel hopeless, isolating ourselves and turning inward can be easy. However, connecting with others facing similar challenges can provide a sense of solidarity and shared strength. Sharing our struggles with others and seeking support from them allows us to find hope when experiencing limitedness.

Although limitedness can lead to hopelessness, it is important to remember that limitations are not permanent. While it may feel as if our options are restricted at the present, circumstances can change. We can often find unexpected ways to move forward by staying open to new possibilities and remaining flexible in our approach. Hopelessness can be a temporary state, and with time and perseverance, it is possible to find hope even in the face of limitedness.

When we feel constrained by circumstances beyond our control, losing hope for a brighter future may appear to be an easy way out. However, by focusing on what is within our control, seeking support from others, and remaining open to new possibilities, we can cultivate hope even in the face of limitedness. Hope is a powerful force that can sustain us through even the most challenging of times, and by holding onto hope, we can find a way forward.

Captivity

Captivity is a situation that has plagued mankind for centuries. Whether it be physical, emotional, or mental captivity, the feeling of being trapped and hopeless can consume one's entire being.

Captivity as a form of hopelessness is explored in various forms of literature, art, and philosophy, representing a fundamental aspect of the human condition. Captivity can manifest in many different forms, from physical imprisonment to emotional captivity within one's mind.

In both cases, the feeling of being trapped and unable to escape can lead to a sense of hopelessness that may be overwhelming. Physical captivity, such as being held in a prison or confined to a specific location, can strip people of their freedom and autonomy, leaving them feeling powerless and hopeless.

Similarly, emotional captivity, such as being trapped in a toxic relationship or struggling with mental health issues, can make individuals feel trapped and unable to break free from their circumstances.

One of the most famous examples of captivity as a form of hopelessness is the story of Prometheus from Greek mythology. Prometheus was a Titan who defied the gods by stealing fire and giving it to humanity. As punishment, Prometheus was chained to a rock where an eagle came every day to eat his liver, which would then regenerate overnight. Prometheus was trapped in this cycle of suffering for eternity. That symbolises the hopelessness that can come from being held captive against one's will. In the modern world, captivity takes on many different forms, from physical imprisonment to emotional and mental captivity.

The rise of technology and social media has created new forms of captivity, where people are constantly bombarded with information and expectations that can feel suffocating and overwhelming.

The pressure to conform to societal norms and expectations can create a sense of captivity, leaving people feeling hopeless and trapped in a cycle of conformity. The experience of captivity as a form of hopelessness may vary depending on the individual and their circumstances. For some, the feeling of being trapped and powerless can be a crushing weight, making it difficult to see a way out.

For others, captivity can be a source of strength and resilience as they find ways to cope with their circumstances and maintain a sense of hope in the face of adversity. Whether it be physical, emotional, or mental captivity, the feeling of being trapped and hopeless can have a profound impact on one's sense of self and well-being. By acknowledging how captivity can lead to feelings of hopelessness, we can work towards creating a more compassionate and empathetic society that values freedom and autonomy for all.

Doom

Doom, a sense of impending disaster or destruction, is often associated with hopelessness and despair. In many contexts, doom is seen as an opposing force that can lead to feelings of helplessness and resignation. However, a paradoxical aspect of doom suggests it can also serve as a form of hopelessness. Doom is often portrayed in literature, film, and other forms of media as a powerful force that threatens to overwhelm individuals and societies. The impending disaster can create a feeling of hopelessness as people struggle to find meaning and purpose in the face of overwhelming odds. In this context, doom can be seen as a form of hopelessness that leads to feelings of resignation and despair.

One of the key aspects of doom as a form of hopelessness is its sense of inevitability. When individuals are faced with an insurmountable threat, they may feel that there is no way to escape or overcome it. This sense of inevitability can lead to a sense of hopelessness, as people believe that because their efforts appear futile, there is no point in trying to change their circumstances.

Doom can also be a self-fulfilling prophecy, as individuals who think they are doomed may act in ways that contribute to their downfall. This can create a cycle of hopelessness, as people become trapped in a mindset that reinforces their negative beliefs and prevents them from taking positive action to improve their situation.

In a broader sense, doom as a form of hopelessness can have profound societal implications. When large segments of the population feel that their future is bleak and that there is no hope for improvement, it can lead to social unrest, political instability, and a breakdown of social cohesion. This can create a vicious cycle in which feelings of hopelessness and despair are perpetuated, leading to further social and economic decline.

Doom can be seen as a form of hopelessness manifesting in resignation, sadness, and helplessness. When individuals and societies face overwhelming threats and challenges, it is not easy to maintain a sense of hope and optimism. However, it is essential to recognise that doom is not inevitable and that there are always opportunities for positive change and growth. By acknowledging doom's role in shaping our perceptions and actions, we can work towards creating a more hopeful and resilient society.

Discrimination

Discrimination, in its many forms, is a pervasive issue that continues to affect individuals and communities across the globe. It is a practice that has been ingrained in society for centuries and continues to be a source of hopelessness for those subjected to its effects. Discrimination can take on many forms, whether based on race, gender, religion, sexual orientation, or other factors, and it can have devastating consequences for those who experience it.

One of the most significant ways that discrimination manifests as a form of hopelessness is through the systemic barriers it creates for marginalised groups. When individuals are discriminated against based on factors such as race or gender, they are often denied access to opportunities that their peers may take for granted. This can include limited educational and employment opportunities, unequal access to healthcare, and social exclusion.

As a result, individuals who experience discrimination may feel trapped in a cycle of poverty and despair, unable to break free from the barriers that have been placed in their way. Discrimination can also lead to hopelessness by eroding an individual's sense of self-worth and dignity. When someone is constantly told that they are less valuable or deserving than others because of their race, gender, or other characteristics, it can have a profound impact on their mental and emotional well-being. They may internalise these feelings of inferiority and begin to believe that they are not worthy of respect and dignity.

This can lead to feelings of isolation, anxiety, and depression, creating a sense of hopelessness that can be difficult to overcome. Furthermore, discrimination can have far-reaching effects on an individual's physical health.

Research has shown that individuals who experience discrimination are more likely to suffer from chronic stress, anxiety, and other mental health issues. These factors can contribute to a range of physical health problems, including high blood pressure, heart disease, and other chronic conditions. The ongoing stress of discrimination can also weaken the immune system, making individuals more susceptible to illness and disease.

As a result, discrimination can have a significant impact on an individual's overall well-being and contribute to a sense of hopelessness about their prospects. In addition to its effects on individuals, discrimination can also create a sense of hopelessness at the community level. When marginalised groups are systematically oppressed and denied equal access to resources and opportunities, it can lead to a cycle of poverty and despair that is difficult to break. This can create a sense of hopelessness that permeates the entire community, leading to increased levels of crime, violence, and social unrest. In extreme cases, this cycle of hopelessness can lead to further discrimination and violence against marginalised groups, perpetuating a cycle of despair that is difficult to overcome.

Addressing discrimination as a form of hopelessness requires a multifaceted approach that addresses both the individual and systemic barriers that perpetuate inequality. At the individual level, it is essential to provide support and resources to those who have experienced discrimination, including access to mental health services, education, and job training programmes. Empowering individuals to advocate for their rights and challenge discriminatory practices can help build a sense of agency and hope for a better future. At the systemic level, it is crucial to address the root causes of discrimination and work towards creating a more equitable society for all.

This may include implementing anti-discrimination laws and policies, promoting diversity and inclusion in schools and workplaces, and challenging harmful stereotypes and biases perpetuating inequality. By working together to dismantle the systems of oppression that perpetuate discrimination, we can create a more inclusive and just society for all.

Discrimination is a pervasive issue that continues to impact individuals and communities worldwide. It can manifest as a form of hopelessness by creating systemic barriers for marginalised groups, eroding individual self-worth and dignity, and contributing to physical and mental health issues.

Addressing discrimination as a form of hopelessness requires a comprehensive approach that addresses both the individual and systemic factors that perpetuate inequality. By working together to challenge discrimination and create a more just and inclusive society, we can help break the cycle of despair and create a brighter future for all.

Experience

Hope is a powerful force that drives individuals to overcome challenges and strive for a better future. It gives people the strength to keep moving forward, even in adversity. However, there are times when hope seems out of reach when past experiences have left a deep sense of hopelessness in their wake.

Past experiences can shape our outlook on life and influence our capacity for hope. Whether they be a series of failures, heartbreaks, or setbacks, these negative experiences can leave us disillusioned and uncertain about the future. The weight of past disappointments can be overwhelming, leading to a pervasive sense of hopelessness that can be difficult to shake.

In my own life, I have experienced moments of hopelessness brought on by past experiences. One experience that stands out is when I failed to achieve a goal I had been working towards for years. Despite my best efforts and dedication, I fell short of my target, which caused me to feel defeated and lost. The impact of this failure was profound, affecting not only my confidence but also my belief in the possibility of achieving my dreams. The disappointment lingered, casting doubt over my future aspirations. I questioned whether it was worth pursuing my goals if the outcome was uncertain and potentially disappointing.

This sense of hopelessness was exacerbated by other past experiences ending in disappointment. Each setback reinforced the idea that success was unattainable and that I was destined to repeat the cycle of failure. The weight of these past experiences made it difficult to envision a future filled with hope and possibility. Hopelessness can be a paralysing state of mind, trapping us in a cycle of negativity and despair. It can cloud our judgement, making it difficult to see beyond our past failures and mistakes.

The fear of repeating past disappointments can be a powerful deterrent to taking risks or pursuing new opportunities. The impact of hopelessness can extend beyond our personal lives, affecting our relationships, careers, and overall well-being. It can lead to isolation, low self-esteem, and a lack of motivation to pursue our goals. The sense of helplessness that comes with feeling hopeless can be crippling, making it difficult to see a way out of the darkness.

Despite the weight of past experiences, it is important to remember that all hope is not lost. While it may be challenging to overcome feelings of hopelessness, it is possible to cultivate a sense of optimism and resilience. By reframing our past experiences as lessons rather than failures, we can extract valuable insights to guide us towards a brighter future.

One way to combat hopelessness is to focus on the present moment and take small steps towards building a more positive outlook. Setting achievable goals, practising self-care, and surrounding ourselves with supportive individuals can help us to navigate challenging times and find renewed hope in adversity.

Another important aspect of overcoming hopelessness is cultivating gratitude for the positives in our lives. By acknowledging the moments of joy, success, and growth, we can shift our perspective from despair to gratitude and hope. This practice can help us see past experiences as opportunities for growth and transformation rather than roadblocks to success.

Past experiences do not define our potential for hope. While it is natural to feel discouraged by setbacks and disappointments, it is important to remember that hope is a choice we can make each day. By embracing the lessons of the past and reframing our outlook on life, we can find the strength to move forward with optimism and resilience. Past experiences can indeed be a form of hopelessness if we allow them to dictate our future. However, by actively choosing to hope and reframing our perspective, we can overcome the weight of past disappointments and cultivate a sense of optimism that will guide us towards a brighter future. Hope is a powerful force that can inspire us to persevere through the darkest times, reminding us that no experience is truly hopeless when viewed through the lens of growth and possibility.

This sense of hopelessness I experienced was exacerbated by other past experiences that had ended in disappointment. Each setback reinforced the idea that success was unattainable and that I was destined to repeat the cycle of failure. The weight of these past experiences made it difficult to envision a future filled with hope and possibility. Hopelessness can be a paralysing state of mind, trapping us in a cycle of negativity and despair. It can cloud our judgement, making it difficult to see beyond our past failures and mistakes.

The fear of repeating past disappointments can be a powerful deterrent to taking risks or pursuing new opportunities. The impact of hopelessness can extend beyond our personal lives, affecting our relationships, careers, and overall well-being. It can lead to isolation, low self-esteem, and a lack of motivation to pursue our goals. The sense of helplessness that comes with feeling hopeless can be crippling, making it difficult to see a way out of the darkness.

Despite the weight of past experiences, it is important to remember that hope is not lost. While it may be challenging to overcome feelings of hopelessness, it is possible to cultivate a sense of optimism and resilience. By reframing our past experiences as lessons rather than failures, we can extract valuable insights to guide us towards a brighter future. One way to combat hopelessness is to focus on the present moment and take small steps towards building a more positive outlook. Setting achievable goals, practising self-care, and surrounding ourselves with supportive individuals can help us to navigate challenging times and find renewed hope in adversity.

Another important aspect of overcoming hopelessness is cultivating gratitude for the positives in our lives. By acknowledging the moments of joy, success, and growth, we can shift our perspective from despair to gratitude and hope. This practice can help us see past experiences as opportunities for growth and transformation rather than roadblocks to success. Past experiences do not define our potential for hope.

While it is natural to feel discouraged by setbacks and disappointments, we must remember that hope is a choice we can make daily.

By embracing the lessons of the past and reframing our outlook on life, we can find the strength to move forward with optimism and resilience. Past experiences can indeed be a form of hopelessness if we allow them to dictate our future. However, by actively choosing to hope and reframe our perspective, we can overcome the weight of past disappointments and cultivate a sense of optimism that guides us towards a brighter future. Hope is a powerful force that can inspire us to persevere through the darkest times, reminding us that no experience is truly hopeless when viewed through the lens of growth and possibility.

The Poverty of the Pocket

Poverty, often described as a lack of material possessions or financial resources, can also be seen as a form of hopelessness. People living in poverty usually face many challenges, leading to despair, helplessness, and a lack of hope for the future. One of the main reasons why poverty can be seen as a form of hopelessness is the limitations and barriers that it creates for individuals.

Poverty can restrict access to necessities such as food, shelter, education, and healthcare. Without these essentials, individuals may feel trapped in a cycle of deprivation and struggle to find a way out. The lack of resources and opportunities that poverty entails can lead to feelings of hopelessness and despair as individuals struggle to envision a better future for themselves and their families. Another aspect of poverty as a form of hopelessness is the impact it can have on mental health and well-being. Studies have shown that individuals living in poverty are more likely to experience mental health issues such as depression, anxiety, and stress.

The constant pressure of being unable to meet basic needs, the stigma and discrimination associated with poverty, and the feelings of inadequacy and worthlessness that can arise from struggling to make ends meet can all contribute to a sense of hopelessness and despair. This can further exacerbate the challenges of poverty, creating a vicious cycle of deprivation and hopelessness that is difficult to break. Furthermore, poverty can also be seen as a form of hopelessness caused by a lack of opportunities and avenues for advancement that it presents.

Individuals living in poverty often face systemic barriers that prevent them from accessing education, employment, and other opportunities for personal and professional growth. Without a way to improve their circumstances or break out of the cycle of poverty, individuals may feel resigned to their fate and lose hope for a better future. The lack of social mobility and upward mobility that poverty can create can lead to feelings of hopelessness and resignation as individuals struggle to see a way to overcome their circumstances and achieve their goals.

The consequences of poverty as a form of hopelessness can be far-reaching, impacting individuals and societies. When individuals are trapped in a cycle of poverty and hopelessness, it can lead to a range of adverse outcomes, including poor health, low educational attainment, and limited economic opportunities.

This can create a downward spiral of social and economic deprivation that can be difficult to overcome. In addition, the feelings of hopelessness and despair that can arise from living in poverty can also have a ripple effect on families, communities, and society, leading to increased rates of crime, substance abuse, and other social issues.

Poverty can be seen as a form of hopelessness due to the limitations and barriers that it creates for individuals, the impact that it can have on mental health and well-being, and the lack of opportunities and avenues for advancement that it presents. The consequences of poverty as a form of hopelessness can be significant, affecting individuals and societies in various ways.

Policymakers, lawmakers, and society need to recognise the link between poverty and hopelessness and work towards addressing the root causes of poverty to create a more equitable and just society for all. By addressing the systemic barriers and inequalities that perpetuate poverty, we can help break the cycle of deprivation and despair and create a future where all individuals can thrive and succeed.

The Poverty of the Mind

Poverty of the mind refers to a state of mental and emotional destitution characterised by negative thought patterns, self-defeating beliefs, and a lack of resilience and hope. It goes beyond material deprivation and encompasses a sense of inner impoverishment that can profoundly affect an individual's well-being and quality of life. People experiencing poverty of the mind may exhibit symptoms such as low self-esteem, feelings of worthlessness, hopelessness, and a general sense of inadequacy. Individuals grappling with poverty of the mind may have difficulty seeing their worth and potential, which can hinder their ability to pursue their goals and aspirations. They may struggle with self-doubt, negative self-talk, and a pervasive sense of pessimism that colours their outlook on life.

This state of mind can lead to a cycle of despair, where individuals feel stuck in a pattern of negative thoughts and emotions that prevent them from moving forward and achieving personal growth. Poverty of the mind can also manifest in social isolation and alienation, as individuals may withdraw from social interactions and struggle to form meaningful connections with others. This sense of disconnection can further exacerbate feelings of loneliness and despair, thus creating a barrier to building supportive relationships and seeking help when needed.

Overall, poverty of the mind can have significant implications for an individual's mental health, well-being, and overall quality of life. It is essential to recognise the signs of poverty of the mind and work towards promoting mental resilience, self-esteem, and hope among people who may be struggling with these issues.

By offering support, empathy, and encouragement, we can help individuals break free from the cycle of despair and embark on a path towards healing, growth, and self-empowerment.

Six Signs of Poverty of the Mind - Not Limited
Feeling Unworthy

Feeling unworthy is a significant sign of poverty of the mind, reflecting a state of mental and emotional destitution that can profoundly affect an individual's well-being and self-perception. In the context of poverty of the mind, feeling unworthy often manifests as a pervasive sense of inadequacy, self-doubt, and low self-esteem that colours one's thoughts, emotions, and behaviours. Individuals experiencing unworthiness may struggle to recognise their value and potential, leading to a distorted self-perception that undermines their confidence and sense of self-worth.

This negative self-image can contribute to a cycle of negative thought patterns, self-criticism, and self-sabotaging behaviours, perpetuating feelings of unworthiness and inadequacy. Feeling unworthy can also manifest in relationships with others, as individuals may struggle to assert their needs, set boundaries, and cultivate healthy connections with those around them.

This sense of unworthiness can lead to difficulties in forming meaningful relationships, seeking support, and expressing oneself authentically, further perpetuating feelings of isolation and loneliness. In poverty of the mind, feeling unworthy can be a barrier to personal growth and self-improvement. Individuals who perceive themselves as unworthy may struggle to pursue their goals and aspirations, believing they are undeserving of success, happiness, or fulfilment.

This self-limiting belief can hinder their ability to take positive steps towards self-improvement and may lead to missed opportunities for growth and development. Addressing feelings of unworthiness in the context of poverty of the mind requires a compassionate and supportive approach that promotes self-compassion, self-acceptance, and self-love. By challenging negative self-beliefs, practising self-care, and seeking help from supportive individuals or mental health professionals, individuals can cultivate a healthier self-image and build resilience against the damaging effects of unworthiness.

Feeling unworthy is a significant sign of poverty of the mind that can have far-reaching implications for an individual's mental health, relationships, and overall well-being. By recognising and addressing feelings of unworthiness with empathy and understanding, individuals can break free from the cycle of self-doubt and self-criticism, fostering a sense of self-worth, empowerment, and hope for the future.

A Fear of Success and Abundance

Success is often seen as the goal in life, the pinnacle of achievement that many strive for. However, for some individuals, the fear of success can hinder reaching their full potential. This fear can stem from various sources, such as self-doubt, fear of change, or a lack of confidence.

The fear of success is a psychological phenomenon that can manifest in various ways. Some individuals may fear the responsibilities and expectations of success, while others may fear the unknown or being judged by others.

This fear can be deeply ingrained in one's mindset, stemming from past experiences, societal pressures, or personal insecurities. At its core, fear of success can be seen as a poverty of the mind, as it limits one's ability to envision a future beyond an individual's current circumstances. It creates a mental barrier that prevents individuals from taking risks, pursuing their goals, and embracing new opportunities.

This poverty of the mind can lead to a stagnant mindset, where individuals settle for mediocrity rather than striving for excellence.

Fear of success can harm one's personal and professional life. It can lead to missed opportunities, unfulfilled potential, and regret later in life. Individuals afraid of success may sabotage their efforts, procrastinate on essential tasks, or downplay their achievements to avoid standing out. Moreover, fear of success can also impact one's mental health and well-being.

Constantly living in fear of failure or success can lead to anxiety, stress, and low self-esteem. This poverty of the mind can create a negative cycle of self-doubt and self-criticism, further reinforcing the fear of success. To overcome the fear of success, individuals must first recognise and acknowledge their fears. Self-awareness is key to breaking free from limiting beliefs and negative thought patterns.

Seeking support from friends, family, or a therapist can help individuals work through their fears and gain a new perspective on success.

Additionally, setting realistic goals, breaking tasks into manageable steps, and celebrating small victories can help build confidence and reduce the fear of success. Individuals can gradually overcome their fears and expand their mindset by challenging themselves to step outside their comfort zone and embrace new opportunities.

A fear of success can be seen as a poverty of the mind, limiting one's potential for growth and achievement. Overcoming this fear requires self-awareness, courage, and a willingness to challenge oneself. Individuals can unlock their full potential and lead a more fulfilling life by breaking free from limiting beliefs and embracing new opportunities. Success is not something to be feared but should be embraced as a stepping stone towards personal growth and self-fulfilment.

Passivity

Passivity, the state of inaction or lack of initiative, can be seen as a sign of poverty of the mind. A passive individual tends to be disengaged, indifferent, and lacking motivation or drive. This passivity can manifest in various aspects of life, such as relationships, work, and personal growth.

When passive, people often fail to take control of their circumstances, make decisions, or pursue their goals. This lack of agency can harm one's well-being and overall success. Passivity can result from various factors, including fear, lack of confidence, and a sense of helplessness.

Sometimes, individuals may feel overwhelmed by challenges or uncertainties, leading them to adopt a passive attitude as a coping mechanism. However, this passivity can become a self-perpetuating cycle, as inaction often leads to missed opportunities and further feelings of inadequacy.

Passivity in relationships can lead to dependency, a lack of communication, and unfulfilled needs. When one or both partners are passive, conflicts may go unresolved, leading to resentment and distance in the relationship.

In the workplace, passivity can hinder one's ability to advance in one's career, as it may result in missed chances for growth, promotion, or recognition.

Additionally, a passive approach to personal growth and development can stifle one's potential and limit one's ability to achieve one's goals. A passive mind is often closed off to new ideas, experiences, and opportunities for growth. It may lack curiosity, creativity, and critical thinking skills.

A passive individual may be content to go with the flow without questioning or challenging the status quo. This can result in a narrow perspective and limited intellectual stimulation.

On the other hand, an active mind is curious, engaged, and constantly seeking to learn and grow. Mentally active individuals proactively pursue their goals, solve problems, and seek new experiences. They are open to feedback, willing to take risks, and eager to explore new possibilities. An active mind is a fertile ground for creativity, innovation, and personal development.

Overcoming passivity requires self-awareness, self-reflection, and a willingness to challenge oneself. It involves taking responsibility for one's actions, making conscious choices, and actively pursuing one's goals.

Developing a growth mindset, seeking new challenges, and cultivating a sense of agency can help break the cycle of passivity and lead to a more fulfilling and successful life.

Passivity can indicate the existence of poverty in the mind, limiting one's potential for growth, success, and fulfilment. Overcoming passivity requires a conscious effort to take control of one's circumstances, make proactive choices, and actively pursue one's goals.

By cultivating an active mindset and embracing challenges, one can break free from the constraints of passivity and unlock their full potential.

A Debt Mentality

A debt mentality can be seen as a sign of poverty of the mind, reflecting a lack of financial literacy, discipline, and foresight. It is characterised by a mindset prioritising immediate gratification over long-term financial stability, leading to a cycle of borrowing, overspending, and financial insecurity. A debt mentality can harm one's overall well-being and limit opportunities for growth, success, and peace of mind. Individuals with a debt mentality often view debt as a quick fix for their financial needs or desires without considering the long-term consequences. They may rely on credit cards, loans, or other forms of borrowing to maintain a particular lifestyle or to cover unexpected expenses.

This reliance on debt can create a false sense of security and perpetuate a cycle of living beyond one's means. A debt mentality can also stem from a lack of financial education and awareness. Individuals who are not well-informed about budgeting, saving, and investing may struggle to manage their finances effectively, leading to a reliance on debt to make ends meet. Without a solid understanding of financial principles, individuals may fall into the trap of accumulating debt without a clear repayment plan.

Moreover, a debt mentality can be fuelled by societal pressures and consumer culture, which promote a culture of instant gratification and materialism. Advertisements, social media, and peer influence can create a fear of missing out (FOMO) and drive individuals to overspend to keep up with others or fulfil societal expectations. This constant need for validation through acquiring material possessions can lead to a cycle of debt and financial insecurity.

A debt mentality can also impact one's mental health and overall well-being. The stress and anxiety associated with debt can take a toll on one's emotional and psychological health, leading to feelings of shame, guilt, and helplessness. Worrying about debt can also affect relationships, work performance, and quality of life. To overcome a debt mentality and break free from the cycle of financial insecurity, individuals must cultivate a mindset of financial responsibility, discipline, and long-term planning.

This involves developing a budget, setting financial goals, and prioritising saving and investing for the future. Seeking financial education, resources, and support can also help individuals gain the knowledge and skills to manage their finances effectively. A debt mentality can be a sign of poverty of the mind, reflecting a lack of financial literacy, discipline, and foresight.

Overcoming a debt mentality requires a shift towards financial responsibility, discipline, and long-term planning. By cultivating an attitude of financial empowerment and taking proactive steps to manage one's finances effectively, individuals can break free from the cycle of debt and achieve greater financial stability and peace of mind.

A Small Vision

A small vision can be seen as a sign of poverty of the mind, reflecting a limited perspective, a lack of ambition, and narrow thinking. A small vision focuses on immediate concerns and short-term goals and shows a reluctance to dream big or think beyond the status quo. This constrained outlook can hinder personal growth, limit opportunities for success, and prevent individuals from realising their full potential. A small vision often stems from a fear of failure, a lack of self-belief, or a comfort zone mentality. Individuals with a small vision may hesitate to take risks, step out of their comfort zone, or pursue ambitious goals due to a fear of uncertainty or rejection.

This fear of failure can lead to a mindset of playing it safe, sticking to the familiar, and avoiding challenges that may lead to personal growth and development. Moreover, a small vision can result from external influences such as societal expectations, negative feedback, or lack of support. Individuals discouraged or criticised for their ideas, dreams, or aspirations may internalise these messages and develop a limited belief in their potential. This can result in a self-imposed glass ceiling that prevents individuals from reaching their full potential and pursuing their passions.

A small vision can also be a product of limited exposure to diverse perspectives, experiences, and opportunities. Individuals confined to a narrow worldview, limited resources, or lack of access to education and mentorship may struggle to envision a future beyond their current circumstances. This lack of exposure can create a sense of resignation or acceptance of mediocrity, leading to a mindset of settling for less than one's true capabilities.

Overcoming a small vision requires a shift towards growth, possibility, and abundance. It requires challenging limiting beliefs, expanding one's horizons, and embracing an attitude of curiosity, resilience, and optimism. Setting ambitious goals, seeking out new experiences, and surrounding oneself with positive influences can help individuals break free from the constraints of a small vision and unlock their full potential. A small vision can be a sign of poverty of the mind, reflecting a limited perspective, a lack of ambition, and narrow thinking.

Overcoming a small vision requires a willingness to challenge limiting beliefs, step out of one's comfort zone, and embrace a mindset of growth and possibility. By expanding their horizons, setting ambitious goals, and pursuing their passions with determination and resilience, individuals can break free from the constraints of a small vision and achieve greater success, fulfilment, and personal growth.

Fear of Failure

Fear of failure can be considered a form of poverty of the mindset, limiting one's potential for growth, success, and fulfilment. This fear can manifest as a paralysing force that prevents individuals from taking risks, pursuing their goals, and realising their full potential. It can lead to missed opportunities, stagnation, and a sense of inadequacy that keeps individuals from achieving their aspirations. Fear of failure often stems from a deep-seated belief that making mistakes or falling short of expectations will result in negative consequences, such as embarrassment, rejection, or loss of self-worth.

Societal pressures, perfectionism, or past experiences of criticism or rejection can fuel this fear. As a result, individuals may avoid challenges, play it safe, and resist stepping outside their comfort zone to protect themselves from potential failure. However, avoiding failure can become a self-fulfilling prophecy, limiting one's ability to learn, grow, and succeed. Failure is an inevitable part of the learning process and an opportunity for growth and resilience.

By avoiding failure at all costs, individuals miss valuable lessons, feedback, and experiences that can contribute to personal development and success. Fear of failure can also lead to a mindset of a fixed outlook rather than growth. Individuals consumed by the fear of failure may believe that their abilities and intelligence are fixed traits that cannot be changed or improved. This fixed mindset can hinder one's willingness to take on challenges, learn from setbacks, and embrace opportunities for growth and development.

Overcoming fear of failure requires a shift in mindset towards embracing challenges, learning from mistakes, and viewing failure as a stepping stone to success. It involves cultivating a growth mindset that values effort, resilience, and perseverance over perfection. By reframing failure as a natural part of the learning process and an opportunity for growth, individuals can develop a more positive attitude towards taking risks and pursuing their goals.

Moreover, seeking support from mentors, peers, or mental health professionals can help individuals address and overcome their fear of failure. By building a support network, seeking feedback, and practising self-compassion, individuals can develop the resilience and confidence to confront their fears and pursue their aspirations with courage and determination.

Fear of failure can be seen as a form of poverty of the mindset, limiting one's potential for growth, success, and fulfilment. Overcoming this fear requires a willingness to embrace challenges, learn from mistakes, and view failure as a natural part of the learning process. By cultivating a growth mindset, seeking support, and practising self-compassion, individuals can break free from the constraints of the fear of failure and unlock their full potential for success and personal growth.

A Victim Mentality

A victim mentality is a state of mind in which individuals perceive themselves as constantly being victimised or oppressed by external forces beyond their control. This mindset can significantly impact one's ability to overcome challenges, take responsibility for one's actions, and succeed. Individuals who adopt a victim mentality often see themselves as powerless and at the mercy of circumstances or other people. They believe that they are always on the receiving end of unfair treatment or discrimination, which reinforces their sense of helplessness and resignation.

This mindset can lead to a lack of agency and initiative, as individuals may feel that their efforts are futile in the face of perceived adversity. Moreover, those with a victim mentality tend to externalise blame, attributing their failures and setbacks to external factors rather than taking ownership of their choices and actions. This avoidance of personal responsibility further entrenches the victim mindset, as individuals fail to recognise their role in shaping their circumstances and outcomes.

As a result, they may become trapped in a cycle of self-pity, resentment, and stagnation. Just as material poverty limits one's access to resources and opportunities, a victim mentality can be seen as a poverty mindset that constrains one's potential for growth and success. Individuals who view themselves as perpetual victims may struggle to develop a sense of self-efficacy and resilience, essential qualities for navigating life's challenges and pursuing goals.

Furthermore, a victim mentality can create a distorted perception of reality, leading individuals to magnify obstacles and underestimate their capabilities. This negative self-perception can erode self-confidence and self-worth, making it difficult for individuals to assert themselves, set meaningful goals, and pursue personal development. Overcoming a victim mentality requires a shift in perspective and a willingness to challenge ingrained beliefs and thought patterns. Individuals must recognise that while they may have faced adversity and injustice, they are not defined by their past experiences or external circumstances.

By cultivating a growth mindset focused on personal agency, resilience, and accountability, individuals can break free from the cycle of victimhood and empower themselves to create positive change. Practical steps to combat a victim mentality include practising self-awareness, reframing negative thoughts, setting realistic goals, seeking support from others, and taking proactive steps towards personal growth and development.

By fostering empowerment and resilience, individuals can transcend the limitations of a victim mentality and embrace their capacity for self-determination and success. A victim mentality can be likened to a poverty mindset that hinders personal growth, resilience, and success.

By recognising the detrimental effects of a victim mindset and actively working to cultivate a mindset of empowerment and accountability, individuals can break free from the cycle of defeat and chart a path towards self-fulfilment and achievement. Ultimately, overcoming a victim mentality is a transformative journey that requires courage, self-reflection, and a commitment to embracing one's innate potential for growth and resilience.

Being Taken Advantage of

Being taken advantage of can be a profoundly distressing experience that can evoke feelings of powerlessness, vulnerability, and hopelessness. It is a situation where one's trust is exploited, boundaries are crossed, and one feels used and manipulated. This exploitation can occur in various contexts, such as personal relationships, workplaces, or even within larger societal structures. When someone is taken advantage of, it often involves a breach of trust and a betrayal of expectations. This can leave the individual feeling disillusioned and questioning their judgement and perceptions of others.

Realising that someone has exploited their trust can shatter their sense of security and safety, leading to feelings of vulnerability and helplessness. Individuals may struggle with feelings of shame and self-blame for allowing themselves to be taken advantage of, further exacerbating their sense of hopelessness. Being taken advantage of can also erode one's sense of agency and autonomy. When someone manipulates or exploits another person, they disregard the other person's boundaries and autonomy. This can leave the individual feeling powerless and lacking control over their life and decisions.

The helplessness of being taken advantage of can be overwhelming, leading to deep despair and resignation. Moreover, being taken advantage of can have long-lasting emotional and psychological consequences. It can erode self-esteem and self-worth, leading to inadequacy and self-doubt. Individuals may struggle with trust issues and find it challenging to form new relationships or be open to others for fear of being hurt again. The emotional scars left by being taken advantage of can linger, impacting one's mental health and well-being. In the face of being taken advantage of, individuals must recognise their worth and value.

Seeking support from trusted friends, family members, or mental health professionals can help with processing the emotions and trauma associated with being exploited. Setting boundaries and learning to assert oneself can also be empowering steps towards reclaiming one's sense of agency and autonomy. Being taken advantage of is a distressing experience that can evoke hopelessness and despair. It violates trust and boundaries, leaving individuals feeling vulnerable, powerless, and disillusioned. It is essential for those who have experienced exploitation to seek support, practise self-care, and work towards rebuilding their sense of self-worth and agency. By acknowledging their experiences and taking steps towards healing, individuals can move towards a place of empowerment and resilience.

Bad Leadership

Leadership plays a crucial role in shaping the lives of individuals and communities. Good leadership can inspire, motivate, and empower people to achieve their full potential. However, bad leadership can have the opposite effect, leading to hopelessness and despair among those affected by it. When leaders fail to act in the best interests of their followers, they create an environment of uncertainty, fear, and disillusionment that can have far-reaching consequences. A lack of vision and direction is one of the key ways bad leadership can cause hopelessness in people's lives. Effective leaders can articulate a clear vision for the future and inspire others to work towards common goals.

In contrast, bad leaders may lack vision or have goals that are self-serving or detrimental to the well-being of their followers. This lack of direction can leave people feeling lost and directionless, unsure of where they are headed or how they can positively impact their lives and the world around them. Bad leadership can also lead to feelings of hopelessness by creating a toxic and oppressive work or social environment. Leaders who are abusive, manipulative, or unethical can develop a culture of fear and distrust that undermines the well-being and morale of their followers. When people are subjected to harassment, discrimination, or exploitation by their leaders, they may feel powerless to challenge the status quo or advocate for change. This sense of powerlessness can erode their self-esteem and confidence, leaving them feeling trapped and hopeless in their current situation.

Furthermore, bad leadership can exacerbate existing inequalities and injustices, leading to feelings of hopelessness among marginalised and vulnerable populations. Leaders who prioritise their interests or the interests of a privileged few over the needs of the greater community can perpetuate systemic discrimination and oppression. When people see their leader perpetuating injustice and inequality, they may lose faith in the possibility of positive change and feel resigned to their circumstances.

This hopelessness can damage colleagues and subordinates struggling to overcome barriers to success and fulfilment. Bad leadership can devastate people's lives by creating a sense of hopelessness and despair. When leaders fail to provide vision, direction, and ethical guidance, they undermine the well-being and morale of their followers, leading to feelings of powerlessness, fear, and disillusionment. Leaders need to prioritise the needs and interests of their followers, promote a culture of respect and integrity, and work towards creating a more just and equitable society. We can inspire hope, empower individuals, and build a brighter future for all through exemplary leadership.

Exploitation

Leadership plays a crucial role in shaping the direction and well-being of a society. When leadership fails to prioritise its people's welfare and exploits them for personal gain, it can lead to a cycle of hopelessness among the population. Leadership exploitation can take many forms, including corruption, abuse of power, and neglect of the needs of the people. When leaders prioritise their interests over those of the population they are meant to serve, it can result in widespread suffering and disenfranchisement.

Corruption can drain public services and infrastructure resources, leading to a lack of necessities such as healthcare, education, and clean water. This exploitation can create a sense of powerlessness and despair among the population, as they see their needs being ignored in favour of the enrichment of a few. The impact of exploitation by leadership on the mental and emotional well-being of individuals cannot be overstated.

When people are constantly subjected to injustice and neglect by those in power, it can erode their sense of agency and hope for a better future. Feelings of hopelessness can manifest in various ways, including apathy, depression, and a lack of motivation to strive for change. When individuals feel that their efforts to improve their circumstances are futile in the face of systemic exploitation, it can lead to a cycle of despair that is difficult to break.

Breaking the cycle of exploitation and hopelessness requires a concerted effort from the leadership and the population that serves them. Leaders must be held accountable for their actions and prioritise their constituents' well-being above their personal interests. Transparency, accountability, and good governance are essential to preventing exploitation and restoring trust in leadership. Additionally, empowering individuals through education, access to resources, and opportunities for participation in decision-making processes can help build resilience and agency in the face of adversity.

How to Deal With Hopelessness

Hopelessness is a familiar feeling that can affect anyone at any point. It is a state of mind where one feels completely overwhelmed, trapped, and devoid of any optimism for the future. Dealing with hopelessness can be challenging, but it is crucial to remember that some strategies and techniques can help one overcome this insurmountable feeling. One of the first steps in coping with hopelessness is to acknowledge and accept the feelings you are experiencing.

It is essential to recognise that it is okay to feel hopeless at times and that these feelings are a regular part of the human experience. By acknowledging and accepting your emotions, you can process them healthily and work towards finding a solution to the underlying issues causing you to feel that way. Another critical aspect of dealing with hopelessness is identifying your feelings' root cause.

Is it due to a specific event or circumstance in your life, or is it a more general feeling of despair and helplessness? By understanding what is triggering your feelings of hopelessness, you can begin to address the underlying issues and work towards finding a solution. Once you have identified the root cause of your hopelessness, it is essential to reach out for support.

Talking to a trusted friend, family member, or mental health professional can give you the guidance and support you need to navigate these challenging emotions. Having someone to talk to who can listen without judgement and offer perspective and advice on moving forward can be invaluable.

In addition to seeking support from others, it is important to practise self-care and self-compassion when dealing with hopelessness. Taking care of your physical and emotional well-being is crucial for maintaining balance and perspective during challenging times. This can include engaging in activities that bring you joy and relaxation, such as exercise, meditation, or spending time with loved ones. It is also important to challenge negative thought patterns and beliefs that may be contributing to your feelings of hopelessness. These thoughts can often be distorted and exaggerated, making the situation feel much worse than it is.

Identifying and challenging these negative beliefs can change your perspective and help you see things more positively. Setting small, achievable goals can also help overcome feelings of hopelessness. By breaking down larger tasks into smaller, manageable steps, you can progress towards your goals and build momentum towards positive change. Celebrating small victories can also help boost your confidence and motivation to keep going.

It is important to remember that feelings of hopelessness are temporary and do not define who you are. It is okay to have bad days and struggle with difficult emotions, but it is essential to remember that things can and will get better with time and effort. By implementing these strategies and techniques, you can work towards overcoming hopelessness and finding a renewed sense of purpose and optimism in life. Dealing with feelings of hopelessness can be challenging, but it is possible to overcome these emotions with the right mindset and support.

By acknowledging and accepting your feelings, identifying the root cause, seeking support, practising self-care and self-compassion, challenging negative thought patterns, setting achievable goals, and remembering that hopelessness is temporary, you can begin to move forward and regain a sense of optimism and purpose in your life. Remember that you are not alone in your struggles and that resources and people can help you through challenging times. With time and effort, you can overcome hopelessness and emerge stronger and more resilient than before.

Steps to Take When Dealing With Hopelessness
Acknowledge the Feelings and Accept

Acknowledging and accepting feelings of hopelessness is crucial in coping with difficult emotions and finding a way forward. While pushing away or ignoring feelings of hopelessness may be tempting, allowing yourself to recognise and validate these emotions can be a powerful tool for healing and growth. The first step in dealing with feelings of hopelessness is to acknowledge their presence and permit yourself to experience them without judgement. It is normal to feel overwhelmed, lost, or uncertain at times, and denying these emotions can only exacerbate your distress.

By acknowledging your hopelessness, you are taking a courageous step towards understanding and addressing the root causes of your struggles. Acknowledging your hopelessness can also help you gain greater self-awareness and insight into your emotional landscape.

By allowing yourself to sit with these difficult emotions and explore their depths, you can uncover underlying beliefs, fears, and triggers that may be contributing to your hopelessness. This process of self-reflection can lead to a deeper understanding of yourself and your inner world, paving the way for personal growth and transformation.

Accepting feelings of hopelessness does not mean resigning yourself to a life of despair or defeat. Instead, it involves embracing your emotions with compassion and openness and recognising them as valid and vital aspects of your experience. By accepting your feelings of hopelessness, you are acknowledging the reality of your current situation and permitting yourself to feel what you feel without trying to change or suppress it. Acceptance can also be a powerful tool for building resilience and emotional strength in adversity. When you accept your feelings of hopelessness, you are willing and better able to confront and work through difficult emotions rather than avoiding or denying them. This willingness to engage with your feelings can foster a sense of courage, determination, and inner strength that can help you weather life's challenges with grace and resilience.

Acknowledging and accepting feelings of hopelessness is essential for healing and growth. By allowing yourself to sit with these difficult emotions, you can gain greater self-awareness, insight, and compassion for yourself. Accepting your hopelessness can increase resilience, emotional strength, and a deeper self-understanding. Remember that it is okay to feel hopeless at times and that by acknowledging and accepting these emotions, you are taking an essential step towards healing and finding hope and purpose in your life.

Hopelessness is Temporary

The feeling of hopelessness can be like a dark cloud that descends upon us, enveloping our thoughts and emotions in a shroud of despair. Just as a dark cloud gathers before the rainfall, hopelessness can loom ominously, casting a shadow over our outlook on life and our sense of possibility. It can feel suffocating, overwhelming, and all-encompassing, leaving us feeling lost and adrift in a sea of uncertainty. When hopelessness settles in like a dark cloud, seeing beyond the immediate storm within us can be challenging.

We may feel trapped in a cycle of negative thoughts and emotions, unable to break free from the grip of despair. The weight of hopelessness can be paralysing, making it hard to muster the strength and motivation to move forward. In moments of profound hopelessness, it cannot be easy to envision a brighter future or to believe that things will ever improve. The darkness of despair can obscure our vision, making it hard to see the light at the end of the tunnel. It can feel as though the rain will never come to wash away the heavy gloom in the air.

However, just as a dark cloud eventually gives way to rainfall, hopelessness can be temporary, too. It is important to remember that feelings of despair are not permanent and that there is always potential for change and renewal. Like the cleansing rain that follows a storm, hope can wash away the darkness of hopelessness and bring clarity and renewal.

Seeking support during times of hopelessness is crucial in navigating through storms. Whether talking to a trusted friend, seeking professional help, or engaging in self-care practices, reaching out for support can help us weather the emotional turbulence and find our way back to a place of hope and resilience.

During hopelessness, it is essential to hold onto the belief that the rain will eventually come, bringing a sense of renewal and growth. Just as the dark cloud before the rainfall is a temporary phenomenon, so is hopelessness, a passing phase that can be overcome with time, patience, and willingness to seek help and support.

Name Your Feelings

Hopelessness is a feeling that can be overwhelming and all-consuming. It is a state of mind where one feels stuck, trapped in a cycle of despair and disillusionment. When faced with hopelessness, finding a way out and seeing a light at the end of the tunnel can be challenging. However, one method that can help individuals cope with hopelessness is by naming their feelings. Naming your feelings is a powerful tool that allows you to acknowledge and address the emotions that you are experiencing. Putting a name to your feelings can bring clarity and understanding to your emotional state. This can be particularly important when it comes to hopelessness, as the feeling can be so overwhelming that it is hard to pinpoint exactly what is causing it.

When you name your feelings of hopelessness, it can help you identify the underlying reasons why you feel that way. It can be a pathway to making sense of the emotions you are experiencing and a way to trace them back to their source. By understanding where your feelings of hopelessness are coming from, you can begin to address the root cause(s) of your despair and work towards finding a solution.

In addition, naming your feelings can also help you to communicate your emotions to others. When we feel hopeless, we often struggle to articulate what we are going through. By putting a name to our feelings, we can more effectively communicate our emotional state to those around us. This can lead to a greater sense of understanding and better support from others, which can help us feel less alone in our feelings of hopelessness. Furthermore, naming your feelings can be a way to take control of your emotions.

When we are in a state of hopelessness, it can feel as though our emotions are controlling us rather than the other way around. By naming our feelings, we can reassert agency over our emotional state. We can acknowledge that we are feeling hopeless but also recognise that this feeling is not permanent and that we can change it. Finally, naming your feelings can be a way to validate and honour your emotional experience. When we are struggling with hopelessness, it can be easy to dismiss our feelings or to try to push them away. However, by naming our feelings, we permit ourselves to feel whatever we feel. We acknowledge that our emotions are valid and that it is okay to experience them.

Naming your feelings can be a powerful method of dealing with hopelessness. By putting a name to what you are feeling, you can bring clarity and understanding to your emotional state, identify the underlying reasons for your despair, communicate your emotions to others, take control of your emotional state, and validate your feelings. So next time you feel hopeless, try naming your feelings – it may be the first step towards finding hope and light in the darkness.

Practise Gratitude

Practising gratitude during times of hopelessness can be a powerful tool for shifting your perspective, finding moments of light in the darkness, and cultivating a sense of hope and resilience. While it may be difficult to feel grateful when overwhelmed by negative emotions, focusing on what you are thankful for can help you find moments of joy, connection, and comfort amidst difficult circumstances. Gratitude is acknowledging and appreciating the good things in your life, whether small or insignificant.

During times of hopelessness, it can be easy to get caught up in feelings of despair, sadness, or frustration, making it difficult to see beyond the darkness. However, by intentionally focusing on what you are grateful for, you can shift your perspective and cultivate a sense of positivity and hope. One of the key reasons why practising gratitude is essential during times of hopelessness is that it can help you find moments of light and beauty within the darkness. By actively seeking out things to be grateful for, such as the support of loved ones, the beauty of nature, or moments of kindness and compassion, you can see the silver linings in your life and appreciate the blessings surrounding you.

Practising gratitude can also help you foster a sense of connection and belonging during times of hopelessness. When you take the time to express gratitude for the people, experiences, and things that bring joy and meaning to your life, you are acknowledging the importance of these relationships and connections. This gratitude can strengthen your bonds with others, deepen your sense of community, and remind you that you are not alone in your struggles. Furthermore, practising gratitude can profoundly impact your emotional well-being and resilience.

Research has shown that cultivating gratitude can increase happiness, contentment, and overall well-being. By focusing on the positive aspects of your life and expressing gratitude for them, you can train your mind to notice and appreciate the good, even in the face of adversity. You can practise gratitude during times of hopelessness in various ways. Keeping a gratitude journal, where you write down three things you are grateful for daily, can help you cultivate a habit of gratitude and shift your focus towards the positive.

Engaging in acts of kindness and expressing gratitude towards others can also help you foster a sense of connection and generosity. Additionally, taking time to reflect on what you are grateful for, whether through meditation, prayer, or simply quiet contemplation, can help you cultivate peace, presence, and gratitude in your daily life. Remember that gratitude is a practice that can be cultivated and nurtured over time, and the more you engage with it, the more profound its effects on your mindset and well-being will be. Practising gratitude during times of hopelessness is a powerful and transformative practice that can bring about positive shifts in your perspective, emotional well-being, and resilience.

By focusing on what you are grateful for, you can find moments of light and beauty in the darkness, foster connections with others, and cultivate a sense of positivity and hope. Remember that even during difficult circumstances, there are always things to be grateful for. By embracing a practice of gratitude, you can tap into the power of appreciation and find a sense of peace, joy, and resilience in your life.

Control

Hopelessness can be a powerful and overwhelming emotion that can consume us in times of difficulty and uncertainty. It can make us feel powerless and trapped in a cycle of negativity, leading us to believe that there is no way out of our current situation. However, in the face of hopelessness, it is crucial to shift our focus towards what we can control and what we have control over. By redirecting our attention to the aspects of our lives we can influence, we can regain a sense of agency and empowerment, thus paving the way for hope to emerge.

One of the first steps in dealing with hopelessness is identifying factors beyond our influence. There are always aspects of our lives that we can manage. This may include our thoughts, behaviours, attitudes, and actions. By recognising and acknowledging the areas where we have agency, we can take proactive steps towards improving our situation. For example, suppose we are feeling hopeless about our career prospects. In that case, we can focus on enhancing our skills, networking with professionals in our field, and exploring new opportunities for growth and development.

We can shift our mindset from despair to possibility and potential by taking concrete actions to improve our professional trajectory. Moreover, it is essential to differentiate between what we can control and what is beyond our control.

We often fixate on circumstances outside our influence, such as global events, other people's actions, or past mistakes. By accepting the limitations of our control and letting go of the need to micromanage every aspect of our lives, we can free ourselves from the burden of unrealistic expectations and unattainable goals.

Instead, we can redirect our energy towards cultivating a sense of resilience, adaptability, and acceptance. By focusing on how we respond to challenges and setbacks rather than trying to control the outcome, we can build inner strength and fortitude that will sustain us in times of hopelessness.

Furthermore, it is essential to remember that hope is not a passive state but an active choice. It requires us to cultivate a mindset of optimism, perseverance, and courage, even in the face of adversity. By nurturing a sense of hope within us and our interactions with others, we can create a ripple effect of positivity and resilience that can inspire change and transformation. Dealing with hopelessness requires a shift in perspective towards what we can control and what we have control over. By focusing on aspects of our lives that we can influence, accepting the limitations of our control, and cultivating a mindset of hope and resilience, we can navigate through challenging times with grace and determination. We can harness our agency and empower ourselves, leading us towards a brighter and more hopeful future.

How Far Have You Come?

Reminding yourself of how far you have come can be helpful when facing moments of hopelessness. Reflecting on your past experiences, the challenges you have overcome, and the achievements you have accomplished can be a powerful reminder of your resilience, strength, and ability to persevere in adversity. Think back to when you faced a challenging situation or felt overwhelmed by hopelessness. Consider the steps you took to navigate that difficult period, the support systems you relied on, and the inner resources you tapped into to keep moving forward.

Acknowledge the progress you have made sense of, the lessons you have learnt, and the growth you have experienced because of overcoming obstacles. Recognise the courage and determination you demonstrated when confronting feelings of hopelessness. Remind yourself of the inner strength and resilience within you and how these qualities have helped you weather storms and emerge stronger on the other side.

By reflecting on how far you have come in your journey, you can gain a sense of perspective and appreciation for your ability to navigate through difficult times. This can instil hope and confidence in your capacity to overcome challenges and face the future with optimism and resilience. Remember that you are not defined by moments of hopelessness but by how you respond to them and the growth that emerges from those experiences. Celebrate your progress, honour your resilience, and trust your ability to continue moving forward, one step at a time.

Healthy Eating

Eating well during times of hopelessness is crucial to self-care and well-being. Maintaining a healthy diet can significantly support physical and mental health when faced with challenges, uncertainties, or feelings of despair. First and foremost, it is essential to recognise the connection between nutrition and mental health.

Research has shown that what we eat can profoundly impact our mood, energy levels, and overall well-being. During times of hopelessness, turning to comfort foods high in sugar, fat, and processed ingredients can be easy. While these foods may provide temporary relief, they can contribute to feelings of lethargy and irritability and worsen mental health symptoms.

On the other hand, a diet rich in fruits, vegetables, whole grains, lean protein, and healthy fats can provide the nutrients needed to support brain function and emotional well-being. Foods such as leafy greens, nuts, seeds, fatty fish, and berries have mood-boosting properties and can help combat hopelessness and despair. Individuals can better equip themselves to cope with difficult emotions and stressors by focusing on a balanced and nutritious diet. In addition to the physical benefits of eating well, maintaining a healthy diet can also help establish a sense of routine and control during times of uncertainty.

When other aspects of life may feel chaotic or overwhelming, a consistent food and meal planning approach can provide stability and empowerment. By making mindful choices about what we eat, we can actively nourish our bodies and minds, even when circumstances may feel out of our control. Eating well during times of hopelessness is a powerful form of self-care supporting mental and emotional well-being.

By choosing nutritious foods, establishing healthy eating habits, and seeking support when needed, individuals can better navigate challenges and build resilience in the face of adversity. Remember that taking care of your body through nourishing foods is valuable for promoting overall health and wellness, especially when hope may feel out of reach.

Make Space to Grieve

Grief is a natural response to loss, whether it be the death of a loved one, the end of a relationship, or the loss of a job. It is a powerful emotion that can leave us hopeless, lost, and overwhelmed. The process of grieving is crucial for our emotional well-being, as it allows us to process our feelings and come to terms with our loss.

When we experience hopelessness, it can be challenging to find a way forward. We may feel stuck in our sadness and unable to see a way out. However, making space to grieve can be a powerful tool for dealing with feelings of hopelessness. By allowing ourselves to feel and process our grief fully, we can begin to heal and find a sense of hope and meaning in our lives. Grieving is a deeply personal and individual process. It looks different for everyone, and there is no right or wrong way to grieve. Some people may find solace in talking to loved ones about their feelings, while others may prefer to grieve in solitude.

Some may find comfort in engaging in activities that bring them joy, while others may find solace in quiet reflection. Whatever form grieving takes for everyone, the key is to make space for it. This means permitting ourselves to feel our emotions, whatever they may be, without judgement or shame. It also means allowing ourselves the time and space to grieve without feeling rushed or pressured to "move on" before we are ready. Grieving can be a messy and confusing process. It may involve a rollercoaster of emotions, from anger and sadness to guilt and numbness. It is important to remember that all these feelings are valid and normal and that there is no right or wrong way to grieve.

One of the most important aspects of making space to grieve is self-compassion. It can be easy to be hard on ourselves when feeling hopeless and lost, but treating ourselves with kindness and understanding is crucial during this challenging time. This means being patient with us, allowing ourselves to take breaks when needed, and seeking support from loved ones or a therapist. Grieving can also be a transformative process.

By allowing ourselves to feel and process our grief fully, we can begin to heal and move forward in our lives. We can develop a deeper understanding of ourselves and our emotions through grieving. We can learn to navigate the complexities of loss and hopelessness with more grace and resilience. Making space to grieve is a powerful tool for dealing with feelings of hopelessness. By allowing ourselves to feel and process our grief fully, we can begin to heal and find a sense of hope and meaning in our lives.

Grieving is a deeply personal and individual process, and there is no right or wrong way to grieve. It is important to treat ourselves with self-compassion during this challenging time and to seek support from loved ones or a therapist if needed. Grieving can be a transformative process, helping us to develop a deeper understanding of ourselves and our emotions and to navigate the complexities of loss and hopelessness with grace and resilience. Making space to grieve is essential in healing and finding hope in the face of despair.

Patience

Patience is a virtue that can be particularly valuable when dealing with feelings of hopelessness. It is natural to feel overwhelmed and frustrated in times of despair. Still, practising patience can help you navigate these challenging emotions and situations with a sense of calm and resilience. When faced with hopelessness, it is essential to remember that change takes time. It is unrealistic to expect immediate solutions or quick fixes to complex problems that may be contributing to your feelings of despair.

By cultivating patience, you can give yourself the space and time to process your emotions, explore potential solutions, and gradually work towards a more positive outcome. Patience can also help you maintain a sense of perspective when dealing with hopelessness. It is easy to become consumed by negative thoughts and emotions, but practising patience allows you to step back and see the bigger picture. Remind yourself that feelings of hopelessness are temporary and that there are opportunities for growth and change, even during difficult circumstances.

Moreover, patience can be a powerful tool for building resilience and coping with adversity. By approaching challenges with a patient mindset, you can develop the strength and perseverance needed to weather difficult times and emerge stronger on the other side. Patience lets you stay focused on your goals, even when progress seems slow or uncertain. In addition, practising patience can help you cultivate self-compassion and kindness towards yourself. It is essential to be gentle and understanding with yourself during times of hopelessness rather than being self-critical or judgemental. By showing yourself patience and compassion, you can nurture a sense of inner peace and acceptance that can help you navigate challenging emotions more effectively.

Patience is a valuable mindset to cultivate when dealing with hopelessness. By embracing patience, you can approach challenging situations calmly, maintain perspective, build resilience, and develop self-compassion. Remember that change takes time, and practising patience allows you to navigate through feelings of hopelessness with grace and strength.

Do Not Overthink It

Hopelessness is a familiar feeling that many people experience at some point. It can be triggered by failure, loss, or uncertainty about the future. When faced with hopelessness, it is important not to overthink the situation, as it can lead to further negative emotions and hinder our ability to find solutions or cope effectively.

Overthinking is a typical response to feeling hopeless, as the mind may become fixated on the perceived lack of options or the severity of the situation. This can lead to a cycle of negative thoughts and emotions that can be difficult to break free from. Overthinking can also prevent individuals from taking action to address the underlying causes of their hopelessness, as they may become overwhelmed by the perceived complexity of the situation.

Instead of overthinking, it is essential to acknowledge and accept the feelings of hopelessness without judgement. It is normal to feel this way sometimes, and it does not define who you are. By allowing yourself to experience these emotions without resistance, you can begin to explore the root causes of your hopelessness and identify potential solutions. One helpful strategy for dealing with hopelessness is to focus on the present moment. Stay grounded in the here and now rather than dwelling on past failures or worrying about the future. Mindfulness techniques such as deep breathing, meditation, or simply focusing on your immediate surroundings can help to calm one's mind and reduce feelings of hopelessness. It is also essential to reach out for support when dealing with hopelessness.

Talking to a trusted friend, family member, or mental health professional can provide a fresh perspective on the situation and offer guidance on how to move forward. By sharing your feelings with others, you can gain valuable insights and support to help you navigate difficult times. It is important not to overthink it when dealing with hopelessness.

By acknowledging your feelings, staying present at the moment, and seeking support from others, you can address the underlying causes of your hopelessness and find a way forward. Remember that hopelessness is a temporary state. With time and effort, you can overcome it and find a renewed sense of hope and purpose in your life.

Staying Present

Hopelessness is a feeling that many individuals experience at some point in their lives. It can be overwhelming and paralysing, making it difficult to see a way out of a challenging situation or a period of despair. However, one way to deal with feelings of hopelessness is to practice staying present in the moment. By focusing on the here and now, individuals can cultivate inner peace and resilience that can help them to navigate challenging times.

One of the main reasons staying present can be an effective tool in dealing with hopelessness is that it allows individuals to let go of worries about the future or regrets about the past. When we are constantly preoccupied with what has happened or what might happen, it can be easy to feel overwhelmed and get stuck in a cycle of negative thinking. By bringing our awareness to the present moment, we can let go of these thoughts and focus on what is happening now. Practising mindfulness is one way to cultivate a sense of present moment awareness.

Mindfulness involves focusing on our thoughts, feelings, and sensations without judgement. Doing so can make us more aware of the present moment and develop greater clarity and calm. This can help us to navigate difficult emotions such as hopelessness more easily. Another benefit of staying present to deal with hopelessness is that it can help individuals build resilience and inner strength.

When fully present in the moment, we can become more attuned to our inner resources and develop a greater sense of self-awareness. This can help us cultivate a sense of inner strength that can sustain us through difficult times. Furthermore, staying present can help individuals develop an understanding of acceptance and compassion towards themselves. We can let go of self-judgement and criticism when fully present and develop greater self-compassion. This can be particularly helpful in dealing with feelings of hopelessness, as it can help us to create a greater sense of empathy towards ourselves and others.

In addition, staying present can help individuals become more attuned to the beauty and joy of the present moment. By focusing on what is happening right now, we can become more aware of the simple pleasures and moments of gratitude that bring us joy and fulfilment. This can be particularly helpful in times of hopelessness, reminding us that beauty and joy can be found in even the most difficult circumstances. Overall, staying present to deal with hopelessness can be a powerful tool for cultivating inner peace, resilience, and self-compassion. By focusing on the present moment and cultivating a sense of mindfulness, individuals can develop a greater understanding of awareness and acceptance that can help them navigate difficult emotions. In this way, staying present can be a valuable practice for building a sense of hope and optimism, even in the face of despair.

Prioritise Meaningful Relationships

It is easy to become overwhelmed and hopeless in today's fast-paced and often chaotic world. Whether due to personal struggles, global crises, or simply the daily stresses of life, it is essential to have healthy coping mechanisms to navigate these challenging times. One such coping mechanism that can be particularly effective is prioritising meaningful relationships. Meaningful relationships are those connections in our lives that bring us joy, comfort, and a sense of belonging.

These relationships can be with family members, friends, romantic partners, or colleagues. What makes them meaningful is the depth of connection and understanding between individuals and shared support and love. When prioritising these relationships, we can find solace and strength in times of hopelessness. When we have strong and meaningful relationships, we have a support system that we can lean on when times get tough. Whether it be a listening ear, a shoulder to cry on, or words of encouragement, our loved ones can offer us the comfort and reassurance we need to keep going.

Knowing that we are not alone in our struggles can help alleviate feelings of hopelessness and remind us that there are people who care about us and are there for us, no matter what. Additionally, when prioritising meaningful relationships, we can cultivate a sense of belonging and connection that can be incredibly healing. Humans are social creatures by nature, and we thrive when we form close bonds with others. By investing time and energy into developing and maintaining these relationships, we can create a sense of community and support that can help us feel more grounded and less isolated when we are struggling.

Furthermore, prioritising meaningful relationships can also help us to find meaning and purpose in our lives. When we have people in our lives whom we care about deeply, we are more likely to find motivation and inspiration to keep moving forward, even when things seem bleak. Whether it be our children, partners, friends, or colleagues, knowing that we have people who rely on us and who we rely on can give us a sense of purpose and fulfilment that can help us combat feelings of hopelessness.

It is also important to note that meaningful relationships are not just beneficial for our well-being. They can also have a positive impact on the well-being of others. By prioritising these relationships and showing up for our loved ones when they need us, we can create a ripple effect of love and compassion that can spread throughout our communities and beyond.

When we take the time to cultivate these connections and nurture them over time, we can create a network of support and love that can help combat feelings of hopelessness and despair wherever they may be found.

Prioritising meaningful relationships can be a powerful form of dealing with grief. By investing in these connections and nurturing them over time, we can find comfort, strength, and purpose in times of struggle.

Whether through the support and love of our family, friends, or colleagues or through the sense of belonging and connection that comes from being part of a community, meaningful relationships can provide us with the solace and support we need to navigate challenging times.

By prioritising these relationships in our lives, we can create a foundation of love and compassion that can help us weather any storm that comes our way.

Reach out for Support

During times of hopelessness, reaching out for support can be crucial in coping with difficult emotions and finding a way forward. Whether you are feeling overwhelmed, lost, or unsure of how to navigate your feelings, seeking support from others can provide comfort, guidance, and a sense of connection. One of the most important reasons to reach out for support during times of hopelessness is to combat feelings of isolation and loneliness.

When you are struggling with overwhelming emotions, you will likely tend to feel alone in your struggles. However, reaching out to friends, family members, or mental health professionals can help you feel less isolated and more understood. Simply knowing that there are people who care about you and are willing to listen can provide a sense of relief and comfort.

Additionally, seeking support can help you gain new perspectives and insights into your feelings of hopelessness. Talking to someone outside your situation can offer fresh ideas, feedback, and strategies for coping with difficult emotions. A supportive friend or therapist can help you explore the root causes of your hopelessness, identify patterns of thinking contributing to your feelings, and work together to develop a plan for moving forward. Furthermore, reaching out for support can help you build resilience and strength during challenging times. By sharing your feelings with others and receiving validation and encouragement, you can overcome obstacles and solve your problems.

Knowing that you have a support system can provide a sense of security and empowerment, giving you the confidence to face your challenges head-on. You can seek support in various ways during times of hopelessness. One option is to reach out to friends or family members you trust and feel comfortable talking to. Opening up about your feelings and experiences can help strengthen your relationships and deepen your connections with others.

Additionally, consider seeking support from a mental health professional, such as a therapist or counsellor, who can provide specialised guidance and support tailored to your needs. If you are uncomfortable talking to someone in person, online resources and support groups can offer a sense of community and understanding. Websites, forums, and helplines can provide a safe space to share your feelings, connect with others going through similar experiences, and access valuable resources and information.

Reaching out for support during times of hopelessness is vital in coping with difficult emotions and finding hope and resilience. By seeking support from friends, family, mental health professionals, or online resources, you can combat feelings of isolation, gain new perspectives and insights, and build a sense of strength and empowerment. Remember that it is okay to ask for help and that you are not alone in your struggles. With the right support system, you can navigate feelings of hopelessness and move towards a brighter and more hopeful future.

Practise Self-Care

During times of hopelessness, practising self-care is essential for maintaining your well-being, managing difficult emotions, and finding comfort and resilience. Self-care involves taking intentional actions to nurture your physical, emotional, and mental health, and it plays a crucial role in helping you cope with challenging circumstances. One of the key reasons why self-care is essential during times of hopelessness is that it allows you to prioritise your needs and well-being. When you are feeling overwhelmed by negative emotions, you may tend to neglect self-care activities and focus solely on your struggles.

However, taking the time to care for yourself can help you recharge, replenish your energy, and build resilience to face your challenges with a clearer mind and a stronger spirit. Self-care also plays a crucial role in managing stress and promoting emotional well-being. Engaging in activities that bring you joy, relaxation, and comfort can help reduce feelings of anxiety, sadness, and hopelessness. Whether taking a warm bath, walking in nature, practising mindfulness meditation, or engaging in creative pursuits, finding moments of peace and serenity can provide a much-needed break from the intensity of your emotions and help you regain balance and calm.

Furthermore, practising self-care can help you cultivate a sense of self-compassion and self-acceptance during times of hopelessness. It is essential to treat yourself with kindness and understanding, especially when you are facing difficult emotions. By engaging in self-care activities that nourish your body, mind, and soul, you can show yourself the love and care you deserve, fostering a positive relationship and building a foundation of self-esteem and self-worth. There are various self-care strategies that you can incorporate into your routine to support your well-being during times of hopelessness.

Physical self-care activities, such as exercise, healthy eating, and adequate sleep, can help boost your energy levels, improve your mood, and enhance your overall health. Emotional self-care practices, such as journaling, talking to a trusted friend, or engaging in creative expression, can help you process your feelings and gain clarity and insight into your emotions.

Mental self-care activities, such as practising mindfulness, setting boundaries, and engaging in activities that stimulate your mind, can help you stay grounded and present in the moment, reducing feelings of being overwhelmed and anxious.

Additionally, spiritual self-care practices, such as meditation, prayer, or connecting with nature, can provide a sense of peace, purpose, and connection to something greater than yourself.

Practising self-care during times of hopelessness is a powerful and transformative way to nurture your well-being, manage difficult emotions, and cultivate a sense of resilience and strength. By prioritising activities that nourish your body, mind, and soul, you can create a supportive and nurturing environment for yourself, allowing you to navigate through challenging circumstances with grace and compassion.

Remember that self-care is not selfish but is essential for overall health and well-being. Investing in yourself and prioritising your needs can build a foundation of self-love and self-care that will sustain you through difficult times and help you find hope and healing.

Talk to a Mental Health Professional

Hopelessness is a feeling that many of us may experience at some point in our lives. It is the feeling of being stuck in a dark place with no way out, no hope for the future, and a sense of helplessness and despair. While feeling hopeless is normal, it can become overwhelming and debilitating if not addressed and managed correctly. One way to deal with feelings of hopelessness is to talk to a professional mental health provider. Talking to a professional mental health provider, such as a therapist or counsellor, can be a helpful and effective way to manage feelings of hopelessness. These professionals are trained to provide support, guidance, and tools to help individuals cope with and overcome their emotional difficulties.

One of the main benefits of talking to a mental health professional is that it provides a safe and non-judgemental space for individuals to express their thoughts and feelings. Many people may feel hesitant or ashamed to talk about their hopelessness with friends or family, fearing that they will be judged or misunderstood.

However, mental health professionals are trained to create a supportive and empathetic environment for their clients, where they can openly discuss their emotions without fear of judgement or criticism.

In therapy sessions, individuals can explore the root causes of their feelings of hopelessness and identify patterns of negative thinking and behaviour that may be contributing to their emotional distress. A therapist can help individuals challenge and reframe their negative thoughts, develop coping strategies, and set achievable goals to achieve a more hopeful and positive outlook.

Moreover, mental health professionals can offer practical tools and techniques to help individuals manage their feelings of hopelessness. These may include relaxation techniques, mindfulness practices, cognitive-behavioural therapy (CBT) exercises, and other evidence-based interventions that are effective in treating depressive symptoms and promoting emotional well-being. Additionally, talking to a mental health professional can provide individuals with validation and validation.

Many people who experience feelings of hopelessness may feel isolated and alone in their struggles, believing that no one else understands what they are going through. However, by talking to a therapist or counsellor, individuals can gain validation for their experiences, feelings, and emotions, knowing that they are not alone in their struggles and that help and support are available.

Furthermore, mental health professionals can help individuals build a support network and connect them with other resources and services that may be beneficial in managing their feelings of hopelessness.

This may include referrals to support groups, medication management, community resources, and other mental health professionals who can provide specialised care and treatment. Talking to a professional mental health provider can be a valuable and effective way for individuals to deal with feelings of hopelessness and regain a sense of hope and well-being.

By providing a safe and non-judgemental space, exploring the root causes of emotional distress, offering practical tools and techniques, and providing validation and support, mental health professionals can help individuals cope with their feelings of hopelessness and work towards a more positive and hopeful future. If you or someone you know is struggling with feelings of hopelessness, do not hesitate to reach out to a mental health professional for support and guidance. Remember, there is always hope and help available.

Motivation on How to Deal With Hopelessness

Hopelessness is a feeling that can weigh heavily on an individual, leading to a sense of despair and helplessness. It is often accompanied by feelings of sadness, anxiety, and a lack of motivation. When someone is experiencing hopelessness, it can be difficult to see a way out of their current situation or to believe that things will get better. One common source of hopelessness is depression, a mental health condition that affects millions of people worldwide.

Depression can make it challenging to find joy in life, leading to a sense of hopelessness and despair. Similarly, anxiety can also contribute to feelings of hopelessness, as constant worry and fear can overshadow any sense of optimism or positivity. For those struggling with hopelessness, it is essential to remember that there is always hope, even in the darkest of times.

While it may be challenging to see a way out of your current situation, reaching out for help and support is crucial. Whether talking to a friend, family member, therapist, or counsellor, seeking help is vital for overcoming feelings of hopelessness.

Additionally, practising self-care and self-compassion can also help combat feelings of hopelessness. Engaging in activities that bring you joy, such as exercise, hobbies, or spending time with loved ones, can help lift your spirits and remind you that there is still beauty and happiness in the world. Taking care of your physical and mental health is essential in combating hopelessness and despair.

It is also important to remember that feelings of hopelessness are temporary and that they do not define you as a person. You are not alone in your struggles; some people care about you and want to help you through difficult times. Reach out for support, practice self-care, and remember there is always hope for a brighter tomorrow.

Hopelessness is challenging to navigate, but it is essential to remember that there is always hope. Whether you are struggling with depression, anxiety, or any other mental health condition, reaching out for help and practising self-care are crucial steps in overcoming feelings of hopelessness.

Remember that you are not alone; some people care about you and want to help you through difficult times. Stay strong, seek support, and believe there is always hope for a brighter tomorrow.

Salute!

As you reach the final page of this book, I want to leave you with a message of hope and motivation. In the journey through the depths of hopelessness we have explored together, it is essential to remember that hopelessness is temporary.

It is a passing storm that may cloud our vision momentarily, but it does not define our future or determine our destiny. Just as the darkest night gives way to the light of dawn, so does hopelessness eventually give rise to hope. We discover our inner reservoirs of strength, resilience, and courage in moments of despair and uncertainty.

In facing our fears and doubts head-on, we realise the depth of our capacity to endure and overcome. While hopelessness may cast a shadow over our lives, it is essential to remember that it is not a permanent state. It is a transient emotion that ebbs and flows like the tides, reminding us of the impermanence of all things. By embracing this truth and believing that better days lie ahead, we can find solace in the knowledge that hope is always within reach.

As you close this chapter on hopelessness, I encourage you to carry with you the understanding that every storm eventually passes, every night gives way to a new day, and every moment of despair is a stepping stone towards a brighter future. Embrace the challenges that come your way, knowing they are temporary obstacles that will lead you towards growth, transformation, and renewal.

May this book serve as a beacon of light in your darkest moments, a reminder that hopelessness is not the end of the road but a path towards a new beginning. Keep the flame of hope burning bright within your heart, for it is the guiding light that will lead you out of the shadows and into the dawn of a new day filled with promise, possibility, and endless potential. Remember, dear reader, that hopelessness is temporary, but the strength and resilience you cultivate in the face of it are everlasting. Embrace the journey ahead with courage, faith, and unwavering determination, for the best is yet to come.

Jeremiah 29:11

For I know the plans I have for you," declares the Lord, "plans to prosper you and not to harm you, plans to give you hope and a future."

www.ingramcontent.com/pod-product-compliance
Lightning Source LLC
Chambersburg PA
CBHW072010290426
44109CB00018B/2195